THE WOMAN LOOKED TO BE IN HER MID-THIRTIES...

She was dressed smartly in a cream-colored turtleneck sweater, a tan, belted, three-quarter-length jacket, brown slacks, and calf-high brown boots. Her skin was milky white. Pencil-thin eyebrows curled high above her green eyes. Her auburn hair was clipped short, but stylishly. Her face was soft, warm, and it bore a strong resemblance to the face of actress Shirley Maclaine. It was the face of a mother of two grown children, a daughter, 22, and a son, 19. It was also the face of a woman who earned her living hunting down New York City's most savage killers.

It was the face of Carolann Natale.

HOMICIDE COP:

THE TRUE STORY OF CAROLANN NATALE

by Neal Hirschfeld

BERKLEY BOOKS, NEW YORK

Portions of this book originally appeared in an article titled
"Homicide" in the June 3, 1979, issue of the *Daily News
Sunday Magazine*. Copyright © 1979 by New York News, Inc.
Reprinted by permission.

HOMICIDE COP: THE TRUE STORY OF
CAROLANN NATALE

A Berkley Book / published by arrangement with
the author

PRINTING HISTORY
Berkley edition / December 1982

ISBN: 0-425-05597-3

A BERKLEY BOOK ® TM 757,375

Berkley Books are published by Berkley Publishing Corporation,
200 Madison Avenue, New York, New York 10016. The name
"BERKLEY" and the stylized "B" with design are trademarks
belonging to Berkley Publishing Corporation.

PRINTED IN THE UNITED STATES OF AMERICA

ACKNOWLEDGMENTS

Many contributed toward this effort, but two in particular must be singled out for a special measure of gratitude. Without the help of Lieutenant Herman Kluge, former commanding officer of the Manhattan Detective Area Task Force, and Ellen Fleysher, former Deputy Commissioner for public information with the New York City Police Department, this book, quite simply, never would have been possible. Their support and encouragement were unstinting, from the very beginning to the very end.

Thanks also to Chief of Detectives James T. Sullivan, Assistant Chief Richard Nicastro, Lieutenant Robert Gibbons, Lieutenant Mark Codd, and the editors of the *New York Daily News,* who allowed the author the time to research and write the book.

Last, but certainly not least, the author wishes to thank the members of the Manhattan Detective Area Task Force who accepted him into their midst for three months. They are gentlemen, friends, and damn fine cops, each and every one.

AUTHOR'S NOTE

The events in this book are based upon true incidents. Some facts have been changed, principally to disguise the locations of crime scenes and the identities and addresses of victims. Most of the police officers, detectives, and superior officers appear as themselves, but the names of others have been changed out of respect for their privacy. Similarly, the names of most victims, witnesses, suspects, and defendants have been fictionalized.

PART ONE

To Catch a Killer

INTRODUCTION

Homicide.

A chilling word, considering that in 1980 more than eighteen hundred unfortunate New Yorkers fell victim to this heinous crime. That was an all-time record, more than six times the number of people murdered in the city in 1939.

For detectives of the New York City Police Department, the word homicide had many associations. And none of them was very pretty.

To work homicide was to view corpses that had been riddled with bullets, hacked apart like slabs of beef, or mangled so savagely with tire irons, baseball bats, or claw hammers that they no longer even resembled human forms.

To work homicide was to tiptoe down a dark alley with your revolver drawn, your heart racing wildly and your brain calculating that any moment a crazed killer might leap out of the shadows, ready to pump his .45-caliber automatic into any cop within sight.

To work homicide was to grapple with a snail-like court system that often seemed more enemy than ally, giving the criminals no more than a slap on the wrist while effectively handcuffing the lawmen who were trying to put them behind bars.

The pay was low. The hours kept changing. The days off were usually lousy. And when your time was up and you had to put in your retirement papers, you often didn't have a hell of a lot to show for your twenty years on the job.

Homicide was the kind of nasty, gritty, thankless work that would turn the stomachs of most men. But a woman? The notion seemed foolhardy. A little bit crazy, even.

Those were the thoughts that crossed my mind in late 1977, when I first learned that the New York City Police Department, bowing to pressure for greater equality in the ranks, was about to assign nine women detectives to its crack, all-male homicide squads. As the criminal justice reporter for the *New York Daily News*, I had always been fascinated by cops, the way they talked, the way they thought, the things they saw. But homicide detectives were something special. Tough, crusty, eagle-eyed investigators, homicide detectives were the role models for the Kojaks, the Colombos, the Joe Fridays, and all those other television and cinema supersleuths, none of whom was one-tenth as savvy as the real thing.

Even among uniformed patrolmen, homicide detectives traditionally commanded an extra measure of respect, although it was often given grudgingly. In the old days, when a young patrolman happened on the scene of a murder, he was invariably upstaged by a homicide detective. Pulling to the curb in a battered, unmarked car, the old pro in the dark suit and the creased fedora would ease up to the corpse, whip out his gold detective shield, clamp a hand on the young patrolman's shoulder and condescendingly announce: "Okay, kid, you can leave now. *We'll* take over."

Homicide detectives were a rare breed and belonged to an exclusive club. Men only; no women need apply. Male cops had never really taken to having women in the ranks. But allowing a female to do homicide investigations—well, that had to be the last straw. It was almost like letting a girl play quarterback on a professional football team.

Still, when the police department announced that it would go ahead with its plan to sexually integrate the homicide squads, my reporter's curiosity was piqued. There just had to be a good story here, and I was determined to interview one of the newly named female investigators.

"Why don't you spend some time up in Fourth Homicide?" suggested Richard Nicastro, then a deputy chief of detectives and the executive officer of the Detective Bureau. "They got a woman up there who knows how to handle herself."

Operating out of the Twentieth Precinct on the West Side, the Fourth Homicide Zone was one of the more active squads in Manhattan and "caught" some of the most sensational murder cases in the city. For my purposes, the locale was ideal. But I had my doubts about the subject. What would she be like? A blunt-talking, hard-drinking babe with snake heads tattooed on her forearms and a moustache on her upper lip? Or would she pack a pistol on each hip, another on her ankle, and curse like a Marine drill sergeant? Maybe she'd work out with barbells at the local gym and boast a black belt in karate. Clearly, I imagined the worst.

The Fourth Homicide Zone was everything I had expected. On my first visit, a pair of burly detectives carrying shotguns passed by me, marching a sullen and muttering prisoner toward a lockup cell. Another detective sat puffing on a bazooka-sized cigar as he picked and pecked with a single finger on a rickety old typewriter. His partner, a barrel-chested behemoth of a man who looked like he could pulverize an opponent with one punch, stood off to one side, struggling to adjust the bulging holster under his armpit.

I stepped up to the entrance gate, and an attractive young woman whom I assumed was the receptionist rose from her desk. "Can I help you?" she asked, softly and pleasantly.

Glancing expectantly over her shoulder into the back room behind her, I answered: "I'm from the *Daily News*. I'm looking for Detective Natale."

"Well," said the woman, "You've just found her."

I did a doubletake.

The woman in front of me looked to be in her mid-thirties. She was dressed smartly in a cream-colored turtleneck sweater, a tan, belted, three-quarter-length leather jacket, brown slacks, and calf-high brown boots. A large pendant dangled from her neck. She wore small, gold earrings. Her skin was milky white, smooth and lightly freckled. Pencil-thin eyebrows curved high above her large green eyes. Her auburn hair was clipped short, but stylishly, and her warm, pretty face bore a strong resemblance to the face of actress Shirley Maclaine. It was the face of a mother of two grown children, a daughter, twenty-two, and a son, nineteen. It was also the face of a woman who earned her living hunting down New York City's most savage killers.

The woman smiled, realizing that I had taken her for anything but a homicide detective. This, I was soon to learn, clearly delighted Carolann Natale.

Over the next few days, as I accompanied Carolann on cases and observed her in the office, she regarded me warily. Like most cops, Carolann was tremendously suspicious of the press. But as the only female in an all-male squad, where many of the men were still skeptical of a woman's ability to handle the job, she felt an extra need to be on guard.

Nevertheless, during that first week I witnessed something that convinced me that women had a definite role to play as homicide detectives. It happened at a critical moment in a murder investigation on the Upper West Side. The detectives had learned that a young girl, eight or nine at most, might have witnessed the slaying. But none of them could persuade her mother to bring her in for questioning. That is, until Carolann was assigned to the case.

Imploring softly but persistently, reaching out as one mother to another, Carolann slowly sweet-talked the woman into cooperating. That turnabout, described in more detail later in this book, was the result of a subtle, clever, and totally professional piece of police work. And for me, an outsider, it was fascinating to observe.

Some months later, after Carolann and I had become friends

and decided to expand her story into a book, I asked her to describe what it takes to be a good detective—and, more pointedly, what it takes to be a good *woman* detective. As was her habit, she pondered the question for several moments.

"I'm not a big, tough, strong cop," she answered. "I'm not good at fisticuffs. I'm not gonna duke it out with some guy on the street. I'm just not built that way. If I have to, I'll use my gun. But I still have a place and I still have a function. And I fulfill that function in a feminine way. If I can accomplish the same thing as a man in my own way, that doesn't make it any less valuable.

"Being a detective is not just out on the street, cracking heads and toting shotguns. Being a detective means putting all the pieces together, getting all the information, leaving no stone unturned. Being a good detective is being able to deal with people, good people, bad people. Being a good detective is being able to recognize a situation for what it is. And being a good detective means having a sense of humor, being able to laugh at yourself. The situations you get into—you simply have to roll with the punches.

"Being a woman is a definite asset in detective work. I say, use it to your advantage. And don't be apologetic about it. I'm proud I'm a woman. And I have no qualms about telling the men who make remarks about females, 'Hey, I was a female a long time before I was a cop.' They usually get the message. And I believe that the ones who are fair in evaluating me respect me. The ones who aren't fair—well, it's impossible to have everyone like you."

Carolann candidly admitted that some women detectives defeat themselves. "They have that chip, that attitude. They feel they have to prove themselves and fight for their place. They try to fit into a man's world by acting tough, talking tough, using vulgar language. Maybe some really are that way. If so, fine. But the ones who do it just so they will be accepted by the men . . . well, it usually has the opposite effect. The men see through it. And they resent it.

"Don't get me wrong. I understand that police work is basically male work. I don't fight that. But I like the thought of working in a man's world. I just try to find my own little niche in that world. I get my results my own way. Sometimes I might approach the problem differently, but I accomplish the same thing, without any animosity on the part of the men. That's exactly what I want to do. I'm not a woman's libber. I'm not a pusher. I subtly get the job done and, before the men know it, I've accomplished something and I'm not hurting any male egos, which I'm wise enough to know not to do."

When asked what would threaten their male egos, she replied, "If you accomplished something that possibly a male detective hasn't accomplished. And if you do it in a feminine type of way. The worst thing in the world you can do is brag about it. In fact, the worst thing that any detective can do is go around patting himself on the back. People resent that. A lot of women do it because they feel if they don't do it, nobody else is gonna realize they're there. I don't do that. If I do something good, I just keep quiet and I let somebody else tell people, 'Hey, that was great!' I say, 'Thank you.' And that's the end of it.

"The best thing that can happen to a detective is to be considered capable by his peers. I don't care if it's a male or a female or what. If that happens, if you walk into a new squad and one of the other detectives says, 'Yeah, we heard good things about you, Natale.' Hey, you know, that's the ball game. That's all I ever really wanted."

NEAL HIRSCHFELD

New York City
February, 1981

CHAPTER ONE

With catlike stealth, the woman and two men tiptoed up five flights of stairs, on the track of the most dangerous game.

The woman carried an oversized leather briefcase. Gently, one of the men unscrewed the bare bulb in the stairwell ceiling, killing the light in the top landing that had illuminated the roof of the Brooklyn apartment house like a giant stage.

It was safe now. They pushed open a heavy metal door, peeled away the cobwebs, and stepped outside into the balmy April night. Under the starlit sky, the tall buildings of Manhattan shimmered in the distance. But their gaze was riveted elsewhere, on the windows of the apartment directly across the courtyard, no more than fifty yards away.

"He's in there, I'm certain," whispered the woman. She

was referring to the killer they had stalked for seven months. The man who had led a trio of stickup men on a torture and murder spree in a Lower East Side whorehouse, garroting the manager with an electric cable, puncturing his windpipe with a knife, raping his girlfriend repeatedly, then stabbing her twenty-five times.

Miraculously, the poor woman had managed to survive. Naked and bleeding, clutching only a bedsheet, she had stumbled screaming into the street and collapsed in the arms of a neighbor.

The three on the roof inched toward the retaining wall, crouching low like halfbacks and zigzagging to avoid detection. From the briefcase, the woman pulled out a fat metallic cylinder that looked like a miniature bazooka. It was a night-vision scope to magnify the light from semi-darkened windows, an instrument for sophisticated snooping. She aimed it toward the apartment across the way and squinted through the narrow end. The men peered through binoculars.

Behind the windows, they saw movement. A man in an undershirt flitted by, his face invisible. He sat. He stood. He moved into the next room. Other figures glided into view briefly, then disappeared. Abruptly a window shade shot up and a blurry face pressed against the pane. The three on the roof dropped to their knees, out of sight. They whispered among themselves:

"The guy in the undershirt, he fits the description. But I can't see his face. I don't wanna risk taking the wrong man."

"He always wears a hood and carries his gun on the right side."

"There's probably two guns in there."

"We saw someone who fit the description. We had reasonable cause to go in. So we go in."

"Let's knock on the door. Where's he gonna go, out the window? It's five stories down."

"Let's take him."

The three descended to the courtyard, where they were joined by two more men who had been lurking in the shadows. Composite sketches were passed around. Diagrams were studied, murmurs exchanged. Grim-faced, they headed toward the other building.

A young girl with long black hair walked out of the building. She glanced briefly at the visitors—particularly the woman—then continued on her way, across the courtyard, down the sidewalk, and out of sight.

The woman and four men paused a moment, then headed up the dimly lit stairs... three flights, four flights, five flights. At the fifth floor, they stopped. Quietly, they planted themselves outside an apartment. Revolvers were drawn from concealed holsters. The woman held her gun at her thigh, barrel pointing toward the floor. She stood with three of the men off to the left, ready to spring. The fourth man was crouching directly opposite the door, his gun locked in a two-handed military grip. He nodded to the man nearest the door, who slammed it heavily with a fist.

"Police! Open the door!"

Inside, there was movement. Shuffling feet. Muffled talk. But the door stayed closed.

"Police! Open the door!" they shouted, banging harder.

"Whaddya want?" asked a feeble female voice.

"We're looking for William Coffey in connection with a homicide. Now open the door." One of the men put a gold shield up to the peephole.

"I'm callin' my mother on the telephone," answered the voice, now sobbing with fear. "Mommy, there's police officers at the door and they want me to open it. They don't have a warrant. They showed me a shield. Mommy, what should I do? Mommy?"

The woman outside hissed: "She's stallin'!" The veins in her hand began to bulge as she tightened her grip.

The weepy voice returned: "My mother says if you have a search warrant, put it under the door."

"Her mother must be an attorney," snorted one of the men. "Makes $40,000 a year giving advice."

The woman shouted, "Listen, we don't need a search warrant. This is a felony investigation. We have reason to believe that William Coffey is on the premises. Now open the door or we're gonna have Emergency Service knock it down!"

Suddenly, like the lid on a coffin, the door creaked open. And in they went like commandos, revolvers poised. Four tough, burly men, all homicide detectives—and one tall, trim, remarkably attractive lady, the floral scent of expensive perfume trailing behind her. She, too, was a homicide detective.

Detective Carolann Natale and her team brushed past the plump young woman in the filmy nightgown and fanned out through the four-room apartment in search of the quarry. To the left was the kitchen where a bullet hole in the wall had recently been plastered over. "Looks like her old man took a shot at her," snorted one of the detectives. To the right, a playroom where two small children were frolicking with a menagerie of stuffed animals. They sucked their thumbs and smiled innocently at the big men and the pretty lady with the guns. To the rear, behind some Oriental bamboo curtains, was a living room done in red drapes and red carpeting. Maria, the young woman who had dawdled by the door, now sat on the sofa, wailing like a wounded animal.

In a bedroom down the hall, a young man with a bushy afro, T-shirt, blue jeans, and black ankle-high sneakers sat like a zombie on the edge of an unmade bed, mesmerized by a flickering television set. He seemed totally oblivious to the fact that the apartment had just been raided. He was either incredibly dumb—or a very shrewd actor. But most important, he was not the man they had seen in the window. He was not the killer they had been looking for. The man smiled wanly at the police.

Detective Carolann Natale surveyed the scene and frowned. This was her case, but it had fizzled into a false lead. Natale and the other detectives peeled back the shower curtain in the bathroom, poked the drapes, peeked into closets, and rapped on the plasterboard walls, looking for signs of a secret hiding place. But it was no use, William Coffey was nowhere to be found.

At that moment Maria's sister trekked through the front door, her arms laden with groceries. She was the girl with long dark hair who had left the building just as the detectives were about to enter. Now, seeing them inside the apartment, she flew into a rage: "What the hell you doin' in here! I can't have no guys with guns in here in front of my baby! You don't draw no fucking guns with fucking kids around! I wanna see a search warrant or all-a-yas get the hell out!"

"Shut up!" snarled Natale. "Take her in. Take 'em both in."

Natale turned her attention back to Maria, who was sitting on the sofa, shaking like a leaf. A shopworn hooker, Maria had just been released from the hospital after undergoing a hysterectomy. She was the lover of the fugitive, William Coffey. "You're going to be in a lot of trouble," Natale warned.

Maria, a blimplike figure with bleached orange hair, rocked back and forth on the sofa, moaning: "I just got outta the hospital. You'd be scared too, if all these people with guns came into your apartment."

Suddenly, Natale dropped the "bad guy" pose and was effortlessly reincarnated as "good guy." Kneeling on the floor by Maria's side, consoling, she gently prodded the teary-eyed young woman, asking her if she had seen Coffey. Where had she seen him? Did she see him before she went to the hospital? Did he visit her in the hospital? When did she talk with him? Would she be talking with him again, and how soon?

Whimpering still, Maria picked up the telephone and redialed her mother. "I'm tellin' her, Mommy," she sobbed. "I'm tellin' her. They're never gonna leave me alone, never, never, never. He's gonna kill me!"

Natale eased the phone away from Maria and, like a stern school principal, admonished the voice on the other end. "Now, as a concerned parent, you must tell her it's the right thing to do. She knows where he is. We know she knows. We know he's been here. He can come to my office and surrender. He won't be harmed."

Maria retrieved the receiver: "Let me bring him in, Mommy. I'll bring him in. He's supposed to call me tomorrow at my house. I don't want to hurt him. He won't go by himself. I'll bring him in. He's scared, Mommy, he's scared."

Natale and the other detectives reholstered their guns and moved toward the door. On the way out, Detective Tom Quinn, a white-haired veteran, turned to the two sisters and chirped:

"We'll be quiet going down the stairs, don't worry—and we'll bring refreshments when we come back."

Outside, the raiders concluded that they probably had been recognized by Maria's sister when she left the building earlier to go shopping. She could have telephoned the apartment and tipped off the others, giving William Coffey just enough time to scamper up to the roof and make his getaway.

"Shit!" muttered Detective Natale.

"You had to go in, Carol," Quinn reassured her. "You had to hit it. You had no choice."

"You did the right thing," added Sgt. Bill Taylor. "You can't hit a home run every time."

"You got to third base," offered Quinn. "Don't worry. Maria will bring him in."

In the unmarked radio car on the way back to the squad office, Natale began thinking out loud. "There's no question Maria knows where he is. She's a real good actress, carrying on and on like that. Actresses, both of them."

Unsmiling, her eyes icy, Natale predicted: "He's been holing up like a rat, but he's running out of places to hide. He'll come back. His family is here, his friends. He'll run a red light or something. They're like homing pigeons. They always come back.

"And then we'll get him."

The days turned into weeks, the weeks into months. Still, there was no sign of Coffey.

Seated behind the desk in her office one day, Carolann Natale was playing optimist, bringing the case to a spectacular conclusion—in her head. "I'm thinking positive," she began, a far-off look in her eyes. "I'm thinking he's gonna come out and make a drug buy from the guy in the blue Mercedes. And that blue Mercedes is gonna be full of heroin and cocaine. And my other two perpetrators are gonna be inside the car. And we're gonna grab them all."

"That's pretty good, Carol," remarked Sgt. Pat Breen, the tall, lanky, cigarette-smoking supervisor who wore a perpetual look of having seen it all. "But they'll never believe it in the grand jury."

After the futile apartment raid, a New York City newspaper printed a story about the whorehouse murder in which William Coffey was the prime suspect. At the request of the police department, the paper deliberately substituted a fictitious name for the fugitive to disguise his true identity. The story featured a large picture of Detective Natale, identifying her as one of the investigators on the case.

Publicity often spawns new leads, and Detective Natale received two calls from anonymous tipsters after the story appeared.

One, a female, said that Coffey brutally beat prostitutes who worked for him when he was pimping.

Another, also female, left a more disturbing message. "There's a secret compartment in Maria's apartment," she confided. "All the time them detectives was in that apartment, Coffey was behind a wall . . . jes' lissenin'."

On a muggy July night, Police Officers James Mauritzen, and Daniel McPherson were driving through the Bronx on their way back to the Forty-eighth Precinct stationhouse. Locked in the rear of their unmarked radio car were two prisoners, a man and a woman. The cops had just arrested them for selling drugs.

The police car cruised past the housing projects, past the tenements, past the bodegas. Suddenly, along Crotona Avenue, the officers spotted a group of people gathered on the sidewalk, and fists were flying.

When the police car swerved into a U-turn, its tires screeching, a tall, thin black man bolted from the crowd and began sprinting north.

Officer McPherson jumped from the car. "Halt! Police!" McPherson raced after the black man.

The man ignored the warning and dashed up to a gypsy cab parked at the corner. A middle-aged Hispanic couple was chatting in the front seat, unaware of the commotion on the street. The black man startled them by jumping into the rear seat.

"Get me outta here!" he bellowed. "Move it!"

McPherson was now only a few feet away from the cab. In a frenzy, the black man vaulted over the front seat and tried to shove the woman out the door. He had decided to commandeer the cab.

"Ay, Dios!" screamed the woman, shrieking in Spanish.

McPherson was at the door. The man tried to run for it and

began swinging wildly at the cop. McPherson retaliated with
his nightstick. Pursuer and pursued tumbled to the pavement
in a flurry of fists, arms, and legs. Officer Mauritzen joined
the melee, whacking away furiously with his own nightstick.

The fracas attracted an unruly crowd, many of whom were
openly jeering the cops and rooting for the black man. Mauritzen muscled one of the man's hands behind his back and
handcuffed it. Battered and bruised, he gave up the struggle.
With their new prisoner in tow, the cops headed back toward
their radio car. Only to make a sickening discovery.

Their other prisoners had vanished.

While the cops were preoccupied with the fleeing black man,
the two drug suspects had escaped. The crowd was growing
larger and uglier, taunting the police officers over their loss.
Mauritzen and McPherson radioed a 10-13, the signal to "assist
patrolman." Back-up radio cars were there in minutes to provide
support.

Eventually, the two policemen, disgusted and decidedly embarrassed, managed to hustle their new prisoner into the back
seat of the patrol car. Two good drug suspects down the drain—
all because of a loony who decided to start beating up some
characters in the street.

In the radio car, on the way to the stationhouse, the man
began babbling. "They say I killed a guy in Manhattan."

"What are you talking about?" asked McPherson.

"Goddamned   newspaper   reporter...Detective   Natale
...call Detective Natale, she knows."

Assigned full time to a narcotics detail in the Bronx, Mauritzen and McPherson could not possibly keep tabs on every
homicide that was committed, especially the ones that occurred
in the city's four other boroughs. Still, the unsolicited statement
about a homicide was intriguing. The two officers were careful
not to question their suspect any further until they could bring
him back to the stationhouse and read him his rights.

Back in the squad room, once he had been properly apprised,
they began their interrogation.

"What's your name?" asked the officers.

"Billy the Kid," grinned their prisoner.

He told them a fantastic tale, boasting that he was a pimp
connected with some of the best brothels on the East Coast.

He said he could cast magic spells over the women who worked for him. The cops searched his pockets and found three credit cards and an Ohio driver's license—all stolen.

Billy the Kid began babbling about a murder. "They say I killed someone in Manhattan—you know, Detective Natale and that newspaper reporter..."

The two cops had never heard of a Detective Natale, but after a couple of telephone calls, they learned that there was a Detective Natale assigned to the Fourth Homicide Zone in Manhattan. Anxious not to intrude on a murder investigation, they decided not to question their prisoner any further about the homicide. Instead, they telephoned the Manhattan squad. Detective John Barna was there to take the message:

"Hey, this is Officer Mauritzen up in the four-eight. Listen, we just grabbed a guy up here who you may be looking for. Keeps mentioning one of your people, a Detective Natale."

1:30 a.m.

Carolann Natale lay in her bed, submerged in a deep sleep after finishing an evening tour with the squad. Somewhere off in the distance, a telephone was ringing. The ringing grew nearer, tugging at her like an impatient child. With her eyes still closed, she clumsily groped for the receiver on the night stand. She heard a faintly familiar voice on the other end. Still groggy, not fully comprehending, she hung up the phone, rolled over in bed, and began drifting back into that delicious slumber.

Slowly at first, then like a jolting splash of ice water, John Barna's words began to penetrate. A suspect up in the Bronx...two plainclothesmen had grabbed him...kept talking about a murder in Manhattan...kept mentioning Carolann's name. Carolann's eyes flew open. She sprang up in bed like a jack-in-the-box, flipped on the lamp and called John Barna back.

"I'm on the way."

One hour later, Carolann was walking into the squad room of the Forty-eighth Precinct in the Bronx. There, waiting for her, were Officers Mauritzen and McPherson and Detective Barna, who had driven up from Fourth Homicide in Manhattan after waking Carolann.

Before her sat the man who was responsible for disturbing

her rest. About six feet, two inches tall. One hundred eighty-
five pounds. Close-cropped hair, parted on the left side of the
head. Pencil-thin moustache and a neatly trimmed goatee. He
had a haunted, almost ferocious look in his eyes.

It was that look that did it.

Glancing at the mug shot she had carried around with her
for the last ten months, Carolann had no doubt now, none
whatsoever. You wily sonofabitch, she thought to herself, I
knew we'd get you! The sense of triumph was building, the
adrenalin flowing, and for a moment Carolann felt the impulse
to leap up and give a victory cheer. But holding herself in
check, secure in the knowledge that the killer in front of her
would now be put away for a long, long time, she merely gave
a silent nod to John Barna.

Just then, the black man's eyes widened in recognition. "I
know you!" he blurted out. "I know you! I seen your picture
in the newspaper, Detective Natale. All the time you was up
in that apartment, I was there, I was there. I was hidin' behind
a panel in the closet. I heard every word you said."

Suddenly, the black man grew agitated. "You knew my
name, damn it. You knew my name. Why did you spell my
name wrong in the newspaper, Detective Natale? Why did you
say those bad things about Maria? Why did you get that story
wrong?"

"I didn't write it," Carolann retorted coolly, shaking her
head, smiling a sardonic smile at this incredibly egotistical
criminal. "Blame the reporter."

And then, getting down to business, Detective Carolann
Natale drew up a chair, rolled a standardized form into the
typewriter and began the tedious but necessary paperwork required to officially charge the man in front of her, William
Coffey, with the crime of murder.

CHAPTER TWO

The voice of Luciano Pavarotti soared and swirled from a stereo set, filling the entire apartment with a spine-tingling aria by Verdi.

As the great tenor surged to a mighty finale *con brio,* Carolann Natale leaned back in a reclining chair and hummed along softly, totally and blissfully entranced.

She sat quietly for a few moments, staring out the window at a small sailboat on the horizon of Long Island Sound, then reached for another album.

Sometimes, during lulls on the job, Carolann and Terry McLinskey, the other opera buff in the Fourth Homicide Zone, would sit in a back room and listen to tape cassettes of *Carmen* or *Die Fledermaus* or *Rigoletto*. Murderers and mezzo-sopranos—just the combination to make a homicide detective's day. A fellow Carolann had once dated introduced her to opera, and she had been a devotee ever since.

Pavarotti launched into a melodic rendition of "La donna e mobile," and Carolann closed her eyes, enraptured again. She wore a red silk blouse, tan slacks, and blue powder-puff slippers, for it was Sunday, the detective's day off.

Her apartment was cheerful and inviting, brightened by a colorful collection of oil-painted seascapes and still lifes. Green plants sprouted from pots on the carpeted floors or crept from small cups and bowls on the window sills. Bookshelves were crammed with novels by Twain, Faulkner, Hemingway, and H.G. Wells, plays by Shakespeare, war histories, collected volumes on religion and civilization, travel guides, paperback mysteries, potboilers. And, of course, dozens of stories about cops.

Just as the aria came to a conclusion, Brenda Lee Natale walked into the den. A pretty blonde-haired girl, dressed in designer jeans and high heels, she cut a striking figure. At five feet nine inches, she was a full inch taller than Carolann. It was hard to believe that they were mother and daughter. Brenda Lee was twenty-two, Carolann thirty-nine.

"Mom, what are you going to do with this apartment after I move into my own place?" asked Brenda Lee.

With her son, John, stationed at a Naval base in California and Brenda Lee about to set off on her own, Carolann would be living alone for the first time in her life. There would be lonely moments ahead, of that she was certain. And without Brenda Lee's monthly contribution of two hundred dollars, it would be tougher to meet the rent. But her daughter was no longer a little girl. She had a full-time job as a beautician, her own friends, and a steady boyfriend, and Carolann respected her desire for privacy.

Carolann looked up from the record album she had been considering. "I don't know. I could take on a boarder."

"A boarder? Like who?"

"Like someone six-foot-two, tall, dark, and handsome," said Carolann with a wink.

Brenda Lee began to laugh. "Yeah, yeah, good idea!"

Twenty years had passed since Carolann left her husband and moved to New York City with her children. Since the breakup, she had dated different men, including several cops and retired cops, as well as people in other professions. Male companionship was important to her, but she had shied away from remarrying, even though there had been several proposals.

One suitor, a wealthy construction man, had asked her to quit her job with the police department to become his wife. She had pondered his offer carefully, then decided against it. Abandoning her career would be too great a sacrifice, especially if the marriage did not work.

Jokingly, her girlfriends encouraged her to stay single. "Don't ever get married, Carol," they would tease. "Then you'll be just like us. And the only excitement we ever have is when we hear you talk about your love life!"

Now, though, with the children grown and out on their own, Carolann wondered if she might have a change of heart about sharing her life again with a man.

"Oh, by the way," Brenda Lee was saying, "Johnny called."

"When did he call?" asked Carolann, lowering the volume on the stereo.

"Yesterday. I forgot to mention it."

"Well, what did he say?" Carolann was always anxious for news from her nineteen-year-old son, who was stationed at Alameda Naval Base in California.

"Now, don't get excited—"

"What do you mean don't get excited?" asked Carolann, who was proceeding to do just that. "Tell me what he said."

"See that?" said Brenda Lee. "As soon as Johnny's name is mentioned, you get all excited."

"For God's sake, tell me what he had to say!"

"Well . . . he was playing football with some friends and he tore some ligaments in his knee. They're gonna take care of it Monday at the hospital."

"Oh, gosh, how did that happen? When did it happen? Who was responsible?"

"I don't know, Mom, but he's fine, he's fine, don't worry. He's out partying tonight, having a ball with his friends. He's not worried about it, so why should you be worried?"

"Oh, that boy!" sighed his mother, the detective. "He's gonna turn my hair gray."

At times, Carolann felt guilty that she hadn't been able to spend more time with the children, do more with them. Duty tours on the police force were erratic—sometimes days, sometimes nights, sometimes weekends—and for years a babysitter had cared for Brenda Lee and Johnny while Carolann went off to protect the rest of the city from criminals. Later, as the children got older, they came to understand that their mother needed a job to support them. They accepted the profession she chose and took pride in her accomplishments.

Some of their friends were agog over the fact that Mom could be a cop. "Wow," the girls would say to Brenda Lee. "Isn't it dangerous? Does she carry a gun? Is she stricter than other mothers? Would she arrest you if she caught you smoking pot?"

In reality, Carolann was more liberal than many mothers, but Brenda Lee took pains never to do anything that would cause her mother embarrassment.

The policemother-daughter relationship even had its lighter moments. Once, Carolann went rummaging through Brenda Lee's closet to borrow a white miniskirt, red go-go boots, and a gold chain belt. Then she painted her face with Brenda Lee's lipstick, rouge and eyeliner. And that night, Mother was unquestionably the foxiest-looking decoy to arrest unsuspecting johns in Times Square.

For the most part, though, Carolann had succeeded in keeping the job and her home life separate. She rarely talked shop in front of the kids, and never breathed a word about the dangers she encountered. To the police department, she might be Detective Natale. But to Brenda Lee and Johnny, she was just "Mom."

Over the long haul, Carolann and the kids had managed to work out their problems and make a comfortable life for themselves. Like any normal family, they had their share of spats and squabbles. But despite the disagreements, they remained a threesome, close-knit and loving. For Carolann, who had been forced by circumstances to become both mother and father to the kids, that accomplishment was a source of strength and pride, as well as a consolation.

Not that it had always been that way. In the beginning, there had been many difficult and agonizingly lonely struggles, especially during those bittersweet years of her own adolescence, when she was a young girl growing up in Brewster, New York.

Situated about sixty miles north of Manhattan and a hop, skip, and jump west of the Connecticut border, Brewster is a peaceful little hamlet. With a population of fewer than two thousand, it has six churches, two bars, one all-night diner, and five policemen, a far cry from the twenty thousand-man army that patrols the streets of New York City. Even today, the town has almost a storybook quality to it. There's a street on the outskirts with the improbable name of Peaceable Hill Road. Nearby runs a babbling brook. And nestled along either side of the road are quaint clapboard houses, all with enormous, white-columned front porches.

The downtown area of Brewster, if it can be called that, is centered around Main Street, and it's no more than an eighth of a mile long. A Tudor-style railroad station sits at the far end, and just across the way is Bob's 24-Hour Diner, where Carolann worked as a waitress after she was first married. Bob himself still can be found deftly flipping hamburgers for the noontime customers.

Brewster is a friendly, folksy place, the kind of town where it is perfectly acceptable for strangers to smile and wave to each other as they pass in the street. Nobody bothers to roll up the windows or lock the doors when he parks his car. In Brewster, there simply is no need.

Just past the old Knights of Columbus mansion, long abandoned but still stately, lies Wilkes Street. At the end of this short lane, shaded by giant elms and maples, sits the two-story, red-frame house that once belonged to Sadie O'Hara. It was here, in a cold-water flat on the ground floor, that the young Carolann lived with her family.

Carolann's father, John Walter Jacyn was a strapping six-footer with a rock-hard body and calloused hands toughened by years of physical labor. After coming to this country from

Poland as a young boy, he worked as a railroad man, a lumberjack, a laborer on an upstate pipeline, and a landscaper. He had a zest for life, a boisterous laugh, a short-fused temper and an indefatigable sense of determination and self-confidence, bordering sometimes on thick-headedness and intolerance.

Fishing was John's passion in life and he often had his little daughter, Carolann, at his side as he cast about for trout or bass in the streams and ponds around Brewster. He also loved to tinker with old cars, spending hours taking them apart and putting them back together again.

Soft-spoken and gentle, Carolann's mother, Felicia, was much the opposite of her husband. She was tall and thin and wore her long brown hair tightly braided around her head. At night, she would spend an hour or more in her bedroom, brushing it out into its luxuriant fullness. Felicia seemed to blossom in her later years, radiating an inner beauty that touched both her family and friends. Despite her husband's excesses, she loved him deeply. She was always going out of her way to be kind to those she considered less fortunate, preparing the food for funerals, visiting the sick and the depressed and the elderly, taking it upon herself to listen to other people's troubles. To this day, people who remember her will tell Carolann: "Your mother Felicia—now there was a wonderful woman."

John and Felicia first met when she was sixteen and he was twenty, but it was not until both were in their thirties that they decided to marry. Felicia's parents came from Frosinone, a town of fifteen thousand just southeast of Rome. Although she was born in America and grew up in Utica, New York, Felicia spoke Italian fluently. Like most Italian daughters, she was devoted to her father, Thomas. The old man was a widower, and after Felicia married she insisted on taking him in to live with her.

While this arrangement pleased both father and daughter, it was a constant torment for John. From the very first day, he and Thomas regarded each other with mutual contempt, and would argue with each other at the drop of a hat, jealously competing for Felicia's affections. The two men managed to disagree on just about everything until Felicia would step between them, always the peacemaker.

While Grandpa Thomas could drive John batty, he was the undisputed favorite of Carolann. Six feet, two inches tall, with a full mane of silver hair and an enormous handlebar moustache, twisted taut and waxed smooth at the ends, he cut an imposing figure. Every day, Grandpa would take his constitutional with his beloved granddaughter "Caroleena," hooking the tip of his cane on the back of her tricycle and nudging her along as she pedaled down the sidewalk.

In his heavily accented English, Grandpa would sigh: "Ah, my Caroleena, my walks they get a shorter and a shorter. Alla my friends they die. I no have anyone left to visit."

When they passed Oxman's Stationery, the little girl's eyes would widen like saucers. "Grandpa! Grandpa! Can I have an ice cream cone today?"

"But Caroleena," Grandpa would protest, "I no have a nickel today, no nickel, I'm a sorry."

"Ohhhhh, Grandpaaaa. . . ."

Unable to resist, Grandpa would reach for the little black change purse he always carried in his pocket. "Aha, whatsa this? A nickel! Ah, Caroleena, you lucky girl. Here, go buy youself ice cream cone."

While Grandpa and John were often at each other's throats, they shared a deep and abiding love for the little red-haired girl. Since she was the only child they doted on her shamelessly. It was no surprise that she delighted in being naughty. Once, when her grandfather was giving her a bath, Carolann jumped out of the tub and playfully dashed out the door.

"Caroleena! Caroleena!" shouted Grandpa, searching everywhere. Frantic, he ran to the front porch and looked outside. And there she was, standing right in the middle of the street, stark naked. "Caroleena, why do you do that?" he scolded, and smacked her sharply on the bottom.

Grandpa was the epicure of the household. Using a wooden press that he kept in the basement, he would squeeze grapes to make his own Italian red wine and, on his strolls through town, he would often stop by a field to pick dandelion greens for salads. During the week, when both John and Felicia were out working, Grandpa would start dinner, preparing such Italian favorites as escarole soup, lentils with spaghetti, and *pasta e fagioli*, and a variety of other bean dishes. Beef was rarely served in the Jacyn household because it was too expensive.

They were poor people, and they had to scrimp and save for every nickel. But they tried to accept their poverty with humor. "Our ship is foundering out in the ocean," Felicia would lament. "When will our ship come in?"

And John would laugh: "Looks to me like it's got another hole in it."

Despite the family's financial difficulties, Carolann was a happy child, surrounded by the love and attention of the adults in her life.

But when she turned nine, everything began to change.

After complaining of severe abdominal pains, Felicia was admitted to the hospital for exploratory surgery. The doctors discovered that she was suffering from cancer of the uterus. The cancer was so widespread that they concluded it would be pointless to remove the malignant tissues. Although they never told her, they gave Felicia no more than six months to live.

At about the same time, John also took sick. He had suffered from asthma ever since Carolann was three years old, and his condition flared up again in a series of horrible attacks. While his wife was dying on a hospital bed in the living room, John lay helpless in the bedroom, wheezing and gasping for every breath. A robust man all his life, he was humiliated and embarrassed when his body betrayed him.

Although Felicia suffered terribly, she refused to burden friends or relatives with her anguish. When people came to visit, she would never complain. But at night, when she thought she was alone, she would finally give in to the pain. From the other room, Carolann could hear her mother weeping softly. As her condition worsened, Felicia turned to the church for solace. Every day she would read from the Bible, and she spent hours at a time talking to the priest.

Felicia surpassed the doctors' expectations, living a year and a day beyond her surgery. When she died, she was forty-two years old. Carolann was eleven. Of her mother, Carolann would say many years later: "If there's a heaven, for sure she's in it."

Felicia's death marked the end of the family as Carolann

had known it. With no one able to care for him, Grandpa moved out of the house and went to live out his remaining years with another daughter.

Crippled by his asthma attacks, John was too feeble to hold down a full time job. Occasionally, when he felt up to it, he would work a day or two for a friend who had a landscaping business and tended the grounds of a nearby estate. But after a while John found that even one or two days were too exhausting. To make ends meet, he was forced to go on welfare and move to a cheaper apartment. When Carolann turned fifteen, she lied about her age and began working after high school as a waitress at a tavern. All but a fraction of her earnings were turned over to her father.

In her last year at parochial school, Carolann scored a 95 on her theology examination, second highest in the class and good enough to qualify her for admission to a prestigious all-girls Catholic high school in White Plains, New York. Her father could not afford to send her to a private school, however, so she settled instead for a public high school closer to home.

Despite the disappointment, her freshman year turned out to be an exciting one. There were lots of new friends and a boy on the junior varsity football team whom she had a crush on. She also made the cheerleading squad that year, an impressive feat for a freshman.

But the family's financial situation took another turn for the worse. When the landlord raised the rent, John decided to move again to cheaper quarters. The move put Carolann into a different school district, and she was forced to transfer to a new high school. At the new school she was never quite accepted by the other students as she had been at the first school. She was already troubled by feelings of loneliness, and her sense of isolation intensified.

Her mother was dead. Her father was bedridden with a debilitating disease. Her beloved grandfather was gone. There were no brothers or sisters to talk to. Adolescence, a painful period of change and adjustment for most teenagers, became excruciating for Carolann. There were times when she longed for someone to lean on, someone to protect her.

She began to keep company with a young man who lived

in Danbury, Connecticut. He was older than most of the other boys she had met, already out of school, and he drove a delivery truck for a living. To Carolann he seemed thoughtful and nice and understanding.

One day, on the spur of the moment, Carolann and her boyfriend and another couple drove down to Elton, Maryland. There, they found a justice of the peace who was willing to marry them in a double ceremony. They did it on a lark, nothing more. At sixteen, Carolann became a bride.

When she called her father with the news, he became livid. His voice raspy, his lungs weakened by yet another attack, he warned her: "You made your bed, now you're gonna have to sleep in it." Still, John was unable to fend for himself, and he was quietly relieved when Carolann and her new husband decided to move in with him.

While her husband continued to work as a deliveryman, Carolann quit high school in her junior year and took a job working the counter at Bob's 24-Hour Diner from midnight to 8 a.m. A year later, she gave birth to her first child, a bouncing, blonde-haired girl. The baby was named Brenda Lee.

Another year passed before Carolann began to realize that the marriage had been a terrible mistake. She was a good wife, a dutiful mother, and a devoted daughter to her father. But she felt smothered. There had to be more to life than what she was experiencing. And, already, she was pregnant with her second child.

Late in 1959, John suffered another asthma attack and his condition deteriorated rapidly. For three months he lingered on the critical list at New Haven Hospital. He died in February, 1960. Two weeks after his death, Carolann gave birth to a boy, named Johnny in memory of the grandfather who had not survived to see him born.

It was eight months after Johnny's birth that Carolann announced to her husband that she was taking the children and leaving. On that day, she was twenty years old.

For the first few months after the breakup, Carolann and her little ones stayed with a cousin, Caroline, and her husband, Ralph, who lived in a two-family house in the Bronx. Living conditions were cramped, to put it mildly. Cousin Caroline had four children of her own and, with the arrival of Carolann and her two toddlers, there was barely enough room to turn around. Little Johnny had his crib and Carolann and Brenda Lee slept on the convertible sofa and a cot in the living room.

One day, about a month after the move to the Bronx, Johnny took sick. His temperature began to soar, finally reaching 106 degrees. When his tiny frame began to shudder with convulsions, Carolann rushed him to the hospital. For days he lingered near death, and to Carolann his illness seemed like an act of divine retribution, as if God were punishing her for taking the children away from their father. Even if he survived, the prognosis seemed grim. Neurosurgeons at the hospital discovered that the mysterious affliction had triggered a slight stroke, leaving one side of the boy's body paralyzed. If the convulsions continued, they could cut off the supply of oxygen to his brain, leaving him mentally retarded or permanently disabled.

Weeks went by, but Johnny remained on the critical list. Day and night, Carolann would pace the pediatric ward, praying for some improvement in his condition. Finally, more than a month after she had brought her son to the hospital, his fever broke and the convulsions subsided. Miraculously, the paralysis disappeared. Although only time would tell, the doctors said that they could not discern any permanent damage to his mind or his body. For the first time in nearly six weeks, Carolann was permitted to take her tiny son home.

Soon after, the Natales took up lodgings with another relative, Carolann's Aunt Helen, who also lived in the Bronx. A month later, they returned to Cousin Caroline's building, where the ground-floor apartment had become vacant. Carolann and the kids moved in as tenants. It was their third new home in three months. Only this time, for the first time, it was a home of their own.

To make ends meet, Carolann took a job as a waitress at the neighborhood Italian restaurant, Joe and Joe's. Six nights a week, she would take orders for food and serve drinks from the bar, sometimes staying until five in the morning to take care of late customers. Her salary as a waitress was a meager $15 a week, but with tips and a good weekend crowd, she could boost her earnings to $150 or $200. Nonetheless, money was a constant headache. The rent on her new apartment was $95 a month and she was paying another $200 monthly in babysitting fees, either to her Aunt Helen or a young girl from the neighborhood who would care for the kids while Carolann was working. There was hardly enough money left to pay for routine expenses like food and clothes. Since Carolann could only collect a day's earnings for a day's work, she never dared take time off from the restaurant for sickness or vacation. As the bills began to mount and saving became tougher and tougher, she made up her mind to look for another job. What kind of job, she had no idea.

It was Ralph, her cousin's husband, who first planted the idea in Carolann's mind.

He had been in the profession for years, and the more he talked, the more fascinated Carolann became. It wasn't the novelty or the uniform or some self-righteous notion of law and order that appealed to her, and it certainly wasn't the lure of danger or adventure. In fact, Carolann really didn't know what she would be getting into. In the beginning, the thing that really enticed her was the financial security. A decent salary. Paid vacation and sick days. Medical and dental insurance. A pension at half-pay after twenty years. For a woman on her own with no formal education, no professional skills, and no husband to support her and her two young children, the benefits were undeniably appealing.

It was for those reasons, and those reasons alone, that Carolann first made up her mind to become a cop.

CHAPTER THREE

It was 2 a.m. on the day before Christmas, 1977.

Huddled together in the dead of night, the police officers aimed their flashlights at the sidewalk where the blood had eddied into small pools and was trickling toward the pavement.

The body lay face up, its feet dangling over the edge of the curb. The victim was about thirty-five years old, five-feet-eleven, 155 pounds and wore a heavy black topcoat, brown jacket, brown sweater, long-sleeved green shirt, black socks, black shoes, and black cap. The blood bubbled and oozed from a crimson blossom on the chest and a hole in the back of the head, just below the hairline. One of the officers knelt and felt for a pulse, but there was none.

"Pat 'im down and see if he got any identification," ordered a sergeant, his breath misting into small white clouds in the icy air. The officer who was kneeling found a wristwatch on one arm and a package of cigarettes in a shirt pocket, but nothing else. He looked up at the sergeant and shrugged.

Just then, an elderly man, gnarled and frail, stepped forward. He pulled the collar of his overcoat up around the exposed portion of his neck and studied the corpse on the ground. Sadly, he shook his head. "I know this man."

His English was accented and guttural, in the manner of Eastern Europeans. "His name is Peter Biberaj. He is Albanian."

Satisfied with this unexpected disclosure of the victim's identity, the officers completed the unpleasant but routine task of checking the body.

Once the corpse had been removed to the city morgue, two detectives from the Ninth Homicide Zone in the Bronx drove to the dead man's home in Long Island City to break the news to the next of kin. At the Biberaj apartment, they rang the bell, but there was no answer. They decided to search for the superintendent of the building. When they located the super's wife she reacted to the account of Mr. Biberaj's death with confusion. "There must be some mistake. Mr. Biberaj is visiting his relatives in the Bronx. My husband spoke with him by telephone only this morning."

The detectives exchanged puzzled looks. That telephone conversation would have taken place several hours after the bullet-riddled body was discovered. "May we use your phone?" asked one of the detectives.

He quickly called in the new information and detectives in the office wasted no time tracking down the elderly Albanian who had identified the body in the street. Yes, yes, he admitted, there had been a slight mistake. Peter Biberaj was alive. He himself had seen Biberaj walking around the Bronx that very morning.

For the detectives of the Ninth Homicide Zone—who still had a corpse but no name to go with it—it was back to square one.

The sergeant in the Ninth Homicide Zone peered across his desk at the newest member of his squad and shook his head.

"What the hell am I going to do with her now?" he wondered.

So far, he had managed to keep Carolann Natale busy reading reports, answering telephones and canvassing for witnesses on other detectives' cases, but he didn't know how long he could go on without giving her more risky assignments.

Her baptism in homicide had hardly been auspicious. During the two-week training course conducted by the Detective Bureau, Carolann visited the morgue to witness her first autopsy. Seated in an amphitheater, she watched with morbid fascination as the medical examiner sliced open a corpse with a buzz saw. When he started to do the head, she felt her stomach lurch. He reached into the chest cavity, plucked out an organ with his hand and dropped it into a pail to weigh it. Carolann began to feel nauseous. Just as the medical examiner started to scoop the blood out with a ladle, she jumped from her seat and beat a hasty retreat to the hall outside. The only trouble was that the hall was just as bad as the autopsy room. Bags containing corpses were lying around on rolling tables, and the stench of death hung like a cloud. A ghoulish-looking attendant walked by with a round, pink object in his hands—somebody's head. Carolann took one look, then dashed for the exit.

The male detectives were not very sympathetic to the rookie's plight. After joining the squad, Carolann had to pay a second visit to the morgue with one of her new colleagues. The male detective could not resist a bit of ghoulish hazing. Slipping his hand into a rubber glove, he peeled back the sheet from a murder victim who had been shot so many times that he looked like Swiss cheese. "Hmmmm . . ." said the detective, gingerly poking his fingers into each of the bullet holes, "guess the shots came from this angle." Once again, Carolann headed straight for the door.

To the sergeant, the Ninth Homicide Zone was beginning to look like the local PTA. Not only had they sent him Carolann, but two other female detectives as well. One of them, Hester Bellomo, was Carolann's best friend. They had worked together years earlier as police matrons.

On her first day in homicide, the biggest, gruffest detective in the squad had walked up to Hester and growled: "Lady *you* got a lot to learn!"

And Hester, a petite blonde with dazzling blue eyes, had squeaked back at him in her softest, sweetest, little girl voice: "Well, in that case, I'm sooooooo glad there's a big, strong detective like *you* around to teach me, because if I learn it from you I know I'll learn it right!"

For Carolann the assignment to homicide was a milestone in her career. Homicide was the major leagues, one of the most sought-after assignments in the Detective Bureau. Homicide was the ultimate crime—and the ultimate challenge. To work homicide was to be "top banana."

In late 1977 when the chief of detectives had announced that nine women detectives would be assigned to homicide squads, he boldly explained that women in other detective assignments had shown "tenacity and inquisitiveness—qualities that are especially important in homicide work." Even though some people thought that desegregating the homicide squads was the department's token concession to the women's movement, after ten years on the New York City police force, Carolann Natale had definitely earned her shot. She had paid her dues. So early in 1978, Carolann—divorced mother of two grown children, ex-cocktail waitress and ex-police matron—became a homicide detective.

While this development was a breakthrough for Carolann, it still looked like one big headache to the sergeant in Ninth Homicide. How would the men react to these rookies in skirts? Suddenly, he had a brainstorm.

"Natale, Bellomo. Listen, why don't you two take a run up to 197th Street and check out the addresses on this identity card. See if we got the right name on our DOA this time." That should keep 'em outta my hair for a while, he thought.

The plastic identity card he handed them had been found inside the clothing of the dead Albanian. The cops at the scene had missed it, but the morgue attendants had not. The card identified the victim as Joseph Zadash, a waiter at Mamma Laura's Restaurant.

Carolann and Hester jumped at the assignment. Even though the case had been officially assigned to one of the men, they were itching for action and eager to help out.

They knew that most of the men in the squad regarded them

with skepticism. Men on the job always felt that women were weak and defenseless. But good detective work was more than just a shotgun barrel in the belly or a right to the jaw. It was using your head and playing your instincts. It was getting all the information and putting the pieces together. "Hey, let's stick with this one and solve it," said Carolann in the car on the way up to 197th Street.

Hester Bellomo laughed. Those were lofty expectations indeed for their very first week in homicide.

Joseph Zadash's wife was trying to keep a rein on three small children, who were scurrying about the apartment runny-nosed and bawling, when the two detectives came to her door. Mrs. Zadash was a pudgy young woman with flat, Middle European facial features. Dressed in a drab print housecoat, she wore her long, black hair severely parted down the center and stretched into a taut pony tail. She was fluent in Albanian, but spoke only a smattering of English. Luckily, the detectives found a neighbor who was willing to act as an interpreter.

Carolann and Hester began the interview routinely, inching delicately toward the real purpose for their visit. Mrs. Zadash said she had been worried sick when her husband failed to come home from work early that morning. She had already gone to the police to report him missing.

"When was the last time you saw Joseph?" asked Carolann.

"I saw my husband when he went to work at Mamma Laura's last night," Mrs. Zadash said, with the neighbor translating.

"What time was that?" asked Hester.

"About three o'clock. He called me at five o'clock just to let me know he was okay."

From the neighbor, the detectives learned that the Zadashes, both Albanians, had come to the United States several years earlier from Yugoslavia. Most of their relatives were still in the old country. Their only kin in New York City was Joseph's cousin, Stephen, who also worked at Mamma Laura's. When Joseph disappeared, his wife immediately phoned Stephen for help.

Hester pulled the plastic identity card from her purse. Mrs. Zadash gasped.

"Oh, my God," she sobbed. "He's dead, he's dead, I know that he's dead. Somebody has killed him!"

Carolann placed a hand on her shoulder to comfort her. "Did your husband have any enemies?"

Tears streaming down her cheeks, Mrs. Zadash parted her lips to answer. But she stopped herself short and vigorously shook her head no.

"Mrs. Zadash," said Carolann, "we'd like you to come down to the morgue tomorrow. I'm afraid it will be necessary for you to look at a body."

That night, Carolann and Hester drove from the Bronx to Manhattan to pay a visit to Mamma Laura's. The restaurant was bustling with business during the Christmas season. Harried waiters scurried between tables, serving oversized portions of veal, pasta, eggplant parmigiana, and rich desserts. Businessmen herded together at the bar, where they sipped martinis and ogled the high-heeled young women who passed by, cool and indifferent to their attentions. Out-of-towners, making the ritual sightseeing tour stop at the restaurant, stood obediently in long lines, waiting for tables.

Off in an unused dining room, Carolann and Hester spoke to several of the other waiters who had known Joseph Zadash. Then they talked to his cousin Stephen. Speaking in English, Stephen explained how he had helped Joseph to come to the United States, settle in the Bronx, and find a job at Mamma Laura's, where he worked five nights a week, from 4 p.m. to 2 a.m.

Stephen was a short, gaunt, dark-complexioned man with a wrinkled, weather-beaten face and close-set eyes. He reminded Carolann of a weasel.

"What time did you leave work on the night that Joseph disappeared?" she wondered.

Stephen studied his right elbow for a moment. "Oh, I leave early, around five o'clock," he said, reaching across with his left hand to flick a piece of lint from his sleeve. "I do not feel well, so I go home, take sleeping pill, and go to bed."

"When did you first learn that Joseph was missing?" asked Hester.

"Next morning, when his wife call me and wake me up."

"What did you do about it?"

"I go right to Forty-sixth Precinct in Bronx with his wife to make report of missing person. Then I take subway to Yugoslav consulate to ask help."

Throughout the interview, Stephen wore a somber expression. He already had prepared himself for the possibility that Joseph had fallen victim to foul play. As he explained:

"I used to live in same building as Joseph. But it was very bad neighborhood, so I move out. I tell Joseph many times he must move, too. It is dangerous to walk through dark streets late at night, especially when he carries money."

"How much money could he have been carrying?"

"Maybe twenty, twenty-five dollars from tips he earn at restaurant," said Stephen.

Carolann asked Stephen if he would accompany Joseph's wife to the morgue the following day to view the body.

"Yes, but of course," he answered, with a lack of emotion that neither detective could fail to notice.

Stephen was somewhat surprised to find Detective Natale and Detective Bellomo at the door of his apartment the following night. He had been sitting in the kitchen with his fifteen-year-old daughter, Cimine, when the detectives showed up. They were still curious about why Stephen had left work early on the night of the twenty-third.

Stephen grimaced, as if he had just suffered a spasm, and clutched at his belly with one hand. "Accchhh," he moaned, "I am not in good health. I have much pain from ulcers. I have many operations. I have pain in shoulders and legs, too."

To prove his point, he walked from the kitchen into the bathroom and returned a moment later, juggling half a dozen vials of prescription medicines in his hands.

"I come home early at five o'clock," he continued. "I feel sick. So I take sleeping pill and go to bed."

Carolann spun around in her chair to face Cimine, who had been sitting unobtrusively in a corner. "Do you recall what time your father came home?" she asked the girl.

The girl, an extremely attractive blonde, seemed startled by the question.

"Well," she began, eyes darting toward her father. An unspoken signal seemed to flash between them. "Yes . . ." Again, their eyes locked. "My father came home at five o'clock and took a sleeping pill. Then he went to bed."

"How late did you stay up?" asked Carolann.

"Two, maybe two-thirty. I stayed up with my brother to watch television."

"Did you check on your father while he slept to see if he was okay?"

"Yes," she answered, pausing again to glance at Stephen. "Yes, I checked on him several times, but he was asleep."

"Did he leave the house at any time?" asked Hester.

Another exchange of looks.

"No, no, he never left the house. Not until the next morning when his cousin's wife called and woke him up."

Each time Carolann and Hester asked a question, the pattern was the same. A pause, a darting of the eyes, an uncertain, tentative reply.

"Something isn't kosher," volunteered Hester on the way to the office.

"Someone's lying," said Carolann.

The next day the two detectives drove back to Mrs. Zadash's apartment. They had phoned earlier and learned that the widow, accompanied by Stephen, would be out that morning, making arrangements for Joseph's body to be flown back to Yugoslavia. Cimine, however, would be staying at Mrs. Zadash's apartment to babysit for her three children. This was exactly what the detectives had hoped for—a chance to interview the girl alone, without her father giving cryptic signals from the sidelines.

When Cimine opened the door to the apartment, their anticipation mounted. Both sensed that the case was on the verge of a breakthrough, and that Cimine held the key.

They were disappointed, however, when they discovered that Cimine was not alone after all. Seated on the sofa, looking anxiously at the detectives, were two familiar faces, Mrs. Zadash and Stephen. Stephen had called from the airline office and, upon learning that the detectives were on the way, he rushed back early.

Suddenly, Mrs. Zadash stood up and walked into her bedroom. She returned carrying a bulging black sack, which she handed to Carolann. Inside the sack were a .38-caliber automatic handgun, sixty rounds of ammunition, and two holsters.

"Where did you get this gun?" asked Carolann.

As Mrs. Zadash started to reply, Stephen began muttering angrily in Albanian. He looked as though he were about to burst a blood vessel.

The woman ignored him and answered. Cimine interpreted: "It was my husband's gun. He owned it for about two months. He carried it to work with him for protection."

"Do you ever carry a gun, Stephen?" asked Carolann.

Stephen exhaled sharply, as if he had taken a sneak punch to the midsection. He curled the tips of his fingers to his chest, a gesture that seemed to combine shock with innocence. "Oh, no, no, I never carry a gun. I never even fire a gun."

Carolann wrote out a receipt for Joseph's weapon, and the two detectives tried to question Mrs. Zadash again about Joseph's enemies. But Stephen barged right into the middle of things, flashing the widow evil looks, muttering in Albanian, answering questions before Mrs. Zadash could respond.

This time Carolann exploded. "Will you please be quiet! You are interfering with our investigation. We have to ask these questions. Now let her answer—by herself."

The detectives decided to reinterview Mrs. Zadash the next day. Only this time, they would bring along their own interpreter, a police officer of Albanian ancestry.

From the very outset, Carolann and Hester suspected that Stephen had killed Joseph. Over the next twenty-four hours, there were several developments to confirm their suspicions.

First, the detectives learned that Stephen had a criminal record with the New York City Police Department. Upon arriving in the United States, divorced and the father of two young children, he had "purchased" a new wife, an eighteen-year-old Albanian girl. When the bride tried to run away, Stephen wounded her with a pistol. He would have stood trial for attempted murder, but the young woman mysteriously vanished before she could testify. Police suspected she had been bribed by a friend of the defendant, then whisked back to Yugoslavia. Without a complaining witness, authorities were compelled to drop the charges against Stephen.

Second, immigration records disclosed that before settling in New York, Stephen had been jailed for five years in Yugoslavia. One day, he had come home to find his first wife in bed with another man, a Yugoslavian police chief. So Stephen promptly exercised what he thought were the time-honored rights of a cuckolded husband and shot the police chief dead.

The third development was that Mrs. Zadash ran into a local grocery store and blurted out to two Albanian customers that Stephen had killed Joseph. The two men later flagged down a patrol car from the Forty-eighth Precinct, and the uniformed cops, in turn, quickly notified the homicide detectives of the widow's urgent message.

The fourth thing that happened was that an anonymous telephone caller tipped the detectives that Stephen had killed Joseph because Joseph had impregnated Cimine, Stephen's fifteen-year-old daughter. To the detectives, that information didn't quite add up. Cimine wasn't pregnant. But Carolann and Hester decided that the time was certainly right to round up all the principals in this tangled case—Mrs. Zadash, Stephen, Cimine, and her younger brother—and bring them to the stationhouse so, once and for all, they could get to the bottom of things.

Even before they assembled everyone in the squad office, Carolann and Hester decided on a strategy. Simply put, they intended to squeeze Mrs. Zadash as hard as they possibly could.

The plane that would carry Joseph's body back to Yugoslavia was scheduled to leave in a matter of hours. There was not much time left. Very deliberately, Carolann studied her watch. Then, turning to the Albanian police officer who was acting as interpreter, she told the widow:

"Mrs. Zadash, you've got forty-five minutes to cooperate. Now, either you tell us the truth or you're going to miss that plane. It's as simple as that. You just won't be able to go back to Yugoslavia." She waited for a moment, until the interpreter had finished the translation. Then Carolann asked: "Did your husband have sex with Cimine?"

Mrs. Zadash turned ashen. She looked from Carolann to

Hester back to Carolann again, but seemed frozen into silence.

Hester moved closer to the telephone, ready to call the airport and ask that the flight be held by special police request. She lifted the receiver slowly off the hook and put her finger on the dial. But she would not turn it. Instead, she just looked at Mrs. Zadash. And waited.

"Stephen has threatened to kill me and my children," Mrs. Zadash whispered, clearly terrified. "I know he would kill me if he had the chance."

Hester brushed the dial with her fingertips, but still would not make the call.

Finally, Mrs. Zadash broke down.

Seated in a small room at the Ninth Homicide Zone, where she had been brought by the detectives after her urgent plea for help, Mrs. Zadash recounted a poignant tale of betrayal and revenge, played out on the streets of New York but born of the enigmatic traditions and blood rites of another culture, thousands of miles distant.

It began with the ill-fated marriage of Cimine, Stephen's fifteen-year-old daughter.

Stephen had arranged the wedding with his best friend, whose sixteen-year-old son was to be the groom. In exchange for the beautiful and tender Cimine, the friend made Stephen a traditional offering, $5,000 in cash.

Shortly before the wedding, the girl was sent to live with her cousin Joseph, and his wife, in order to learn to cook and clean and crochet, fitting duties for a young wife. Stephen flew home to Yugoslavia to visit other relatives and inform them of the good news. Upon his return, the ceremony was performed and the newlyweds moved in with the parents of the groom.

On the morning after the nuptials, the parents waited until the young couple had left the house. Then, in keeping with custom, they discreetly made their way to the bedroom and inspected the sheets, searching for traces of virgin blood. But there was none to be found. On the second morning, they repeated the visit. Still, no blood. By the end of the week, there were no indications whatsoever that the marriage had been consummated.

The father finally confronted his young son. "Have you not

h'ad intercourse with your bride?" Yes, the boy insisted, he had. The father demanded an explanation. Sheepishly, the boy admitted that his bride was not a virgin. Joseph, her cousin, had forced himself upon her three times.

The father was furious. He ordered the girl to return to her own home. "You have deceived me!" he told Stephen. "She is soiled. She is dirt. Take your daughter back and return my $5,000!"

Shaking with humiliation, Stephen slapped his daughter across the face, yanked her hair, and then banged her head against the floor. He would have smashed a typewriter over her head had not his girlfriend, who was staying at the house that day, come between them.

The next day, he summoned Joseph to his home for a confrontation. "You must quit your job and leave this country," he hissed at his cousin. "She is our daughter, of the same blood, but you have disgraced me and shamed her. This shame extends to my entire family. As far as I am concerned, this has ended my life. The only thing I want from you is never to see you again. Take your family and go back to Yugoslavia."

But Joseph would not hear of it. He insisted that he had done no wrong. In fact, he argued, the girl had seduced him.

Stephen turned livid. The shame of it all, this stain on his daughter's reputation and his own integrity. He was a man and he would act like a man and, at that very moment, he decided there was only one way left to salvage his honor.

For fictitious homicide detectives, the case comes to an abrupt and tidy conclusion when the murderer is arrested. The tweedy, pipe-smoking inspector from Scotland Yard cocks an eyebrow, spins on his heels, and points an accusatory finger at one of the dinner guests, just as the craven killer is about to take another sip of brandy. Or the muscle-bound undercover cop hurtles headfirst through a plate-glass window, and slaps the cuffs on the killer's wrists. Case closed; tune in next week for a new caper.

But for real-life homicide detectives, arresting the suspect is only the beginning. The real challenge, often more difficult and time-consuming than tracking down the killer, is finding credible witnesses and enough evidence to make the case stand up in court. It may seem less glamorous than making the arrest, but in many ways this part of the investigation is more critical. Sometimes, detectives know who pulled the trigger or who plunged the knife—they just can't prove it.

Once Mrs. Zadash had given her statement, Carolann and Hester knew for certain who the killer was, confirming suspicions they had harbored almost from the outset. But they needed corroboration. And they needed it from the two most vulnerable figures in this tragic blood feud, Stephen's fifteen-year-old daughter and thirteen-year-old son. Cruel and heartless though it might be, the detectives were determined to turn the children against their father.

It was a ruthless strategy, one that hinged on the worst kind of betrayal, and it troubled Carolann to resort to it. She was, after all, the mother of two children, and the bond between a child and a parent had always been very special to her. But she was able to reconcile herself to what she was about to do because Stephen Zadash had been even more ruthless, exploiting his children for his own selfish purposes, bartering off his daughter like a head of cattle, forcing her to provide an alibi for a murder. In Carolann's mind, Zadash was no longer a loving father, only a craven and contemptible killer bent on saving his own skin. Biologically, he might be a parent, but that did not automatically guarantee him the loyalty of his children. So horrendous, so brutal, and so cold-blooded was his crime that any notions of family loyalty had long ago gone by the wayside.

By this time, all the principals in the case had been brought back to the office for questioning. Mrs. Zadash, Stephen, Cimine and her brother were sequestered in different rooms, out of sight of each other. Hester made the telephone call to delay the flight to Yugoslavia, and Mrs. Zadash was permitted to leave for the airport. Now the detectives zeroed in on Cimine, the hapless femme fatale of the crime. They had already started to apply pressure in the car, badgering, shouting, even threatening to lock her up if she refused to cooperate.

Carolann closed the door to the room, and Hester began again: "We know what your father did now, and we know why he did it. If you don't tell us exactly what happened, then you'll be a party to a homicide, too."

The poor girl became hysterical. "I am dead," she moaned. "I am dead. I am dead . . . My father will kill me if I speak the truth."

"Your father can't harm you now," assured Carolann. "We've taken him into custody."

"But you don't understand," sobbed the girl. "It does not matter. If he can't kill me, his relatives will." Albanians neither forgive nor forget, she explained, especially when it comes to betrayals by members of their own family. "Even if they don't kill me, they will send me back to Yugoslavia to marry an old man because I am not a virgin. My life is over either way."

The detectives offered a way out.

Cimine and her brother would be resettled with a foster family outside of New York City, away from Stephen and away from his vengeful relatives. It would mean a new home and a new way of life. No longer would Cimine have to cook and clean and sew for her father, catering to him like a slave until the next time he decided to barter her off to the highest bidder.

Reluctantly, the girl agreed to give a statement. Off in another room, her younger brother was given similar assurances of protection by one of the male detectives. The boy, too, promised to cooperate. And that night their father was formally arrested for murder.

Nicholas Iacovetta, the slim, mustachioed assistant district attorney, called as his next witness "the daughter of the defendant," and the courtroom fell into a hush. Cimine walked slowly up to the witness stand, head bowed, and took her seat. She looked not at the prosecutor nor at the jury nor at the defendant, her father. Instead, she stared down at her feet. Stephen sat with his fingertips glued to the table, shaking his head from side to side, refusing to believe that it was really happening.

Seven months after the murder, the trial had finally commenced. It had been a harrowing wait, especially for young Cimine. She made countless trips down to the Bronx for conferences with the prosecutor and Carolann and Hester, who wanted to go over her story again and again. And always, in the back of her mind, was that lingering fear that some day she and her brother would be targets for revenge.

Extraordinary measures had been taken to protect the children. Arrangements were made by the Bureau of Child Welfare, a city agency, to lodge them in a private home upstate. Even Carolann and Hester were kept in the dark about the identities of the foster parents and where they lived. Whenever the district attorney's office required the children's presence, a call would be made to the bureau. The bureau, in turn, would notify the parents. The parents would have the children wait at a prearranged location, usually a school. There, Carolann and Hester would meet them and drive them to the district attorney's office. At the end of the day, the detectives would return the children to the school and their foster parents would spirit them back to their new home.

The two women detectives tried to befriend Cimine and bolster her courage to testify. Both had daughters of their own and, in some ways, they could offer the girl the strength and understanding that only an older female could provide. In time, the girl learned to be more at ease with them. Now and then, she even shared a laugh.

Then, just as Cimine was first due to testify, her appearance on the stand was postponed. She was returned to her foster home. Her testimony was rescheduled for another day and she was brought back to the courthouse. But again it was postponed. The on-again, off-again course of the proceedings became nerve-racking, almost like torture, and the girl became sullen.

One day, as they were waiting in the prosecutor's office, Carolann asked: "Would you like a hamburger and a milk shake for lunch today?"

"I don't care any more!" snapped Cimine, turning away from the detective.

"Cimine," said Carolann, sitting down beside her on a bench. The girl refused to look at her. "You'll come out of this okay, believe me. You have the courage. You have the strength. It will all be over soon. Once it's over, you'll never have to look back again. You can go on with the rest of your life."

Cimine looked up, tears welling in her eyes, and Carolann

put an arm around her shoulder.

Would the delays ruffle her into recanting her statements? The detectives grew fearful.

Finally, it came time for Cimine to take the stand.

On direct examination, the prosecutor began by leading her slowly through the events of the morning of the twenty-fourth of December, when Stephen had telephoned and asked her to wait up for him. "What happened when you opened the front door?" he asked.

Cimine answered: "When he came in, he said, 'I fucked his mother.' He said, 'You know I killed him.' I said, 'You killed who?' He said, 'I killed Joseph.'"

What else was said, the prosecutor wanted to know.

"Well, I told him, 'Thank God that you are alive,' and then he went to the bathroom and he asked me for a knife and I gave it to him."

"Now, before your father went into the bathroom, did you see him with anything?"

"Yes, with his gun. He took it out of his pocket."

Stephen had used the knife to remove the empty shells. Then he stashed the gun and the spent shells in an umbrella and hid the umbrella on the roof. The next morning, he retrieved the gun and shells, put them in a shopping bag and tossed the bag into a garbage dump behind a department store.

Cimine added: "He said if the police ask anything about this, just say he was sick and went to bed early, he took a tranquilizer."

Moving on, the prosecutor wanted to know what had happened to Cimine when her in-laws had annulled her marriage.

"Well," Cimine said, "they sent me to my father."

"And what did your father say when you told him?"

"Nothing, really. He just got mad."

"When you say he got mad, what makes you say he got mad?"

"Well, because at one time he hit me."

"And did he ask you whether or not it was true that you were a virgin?"

"Yes, he did."

"What did you tell him?"

"I said I wasn't a virgin."

"And did you tell him why you weren't?"

"Yes, I did."

"What did you tell him?"

"Because his cousin raped me."

On cross-examination, the defense attorney tried to probe at Cimine's true feelings for her father. "Do you remember when Mr. Iacovetta asked you and you said that your father came back at approximately three o'clock and you said, 'Thank God that you are alive?'"

"Yes."

"Were you really happy that he was alive?"

"Well, not really—but I was scared that he might shoot me, too."

The defense attorney went back over old ground, the annulled marriage. "There came a time that you were sent back to your father, was there not?"

"Yes."

"When did that take place."

"After about a month."

"Why?"

"Because I wasn't a virgin."

"Did you tell them that you were not a virgin?"

"Who?"

"Your in-laws."

"Well, after they insisted to know, but I didn't just go and tell them."

"What do you mean they insisted to know?"

"Well, the custom is if you don't stain the sheet, they will know that you are not a virgin."

"And then what happened?"

"Then they'll ask you, you know, what happened."

"And what did you say to that?"

"Well, I tried to deny it and I gave, you know, I tried to lie and deny it, but in the end they said that I had to tell or they would send me back to my father and he will kill me."

The defense attorney hadn't quite heard her last few words. "And he what?" he asked.

"He'll kill me," said Cimine.

* * *

The unmarked police car moved quietly along the country
roads, gliding past large, leafy oak trees and manicured lawns
and an occasional pond or stream that shimmered in the summer
sun. Inside the car sat Carolann Natale, the assistant district
attorney, and Cimine.

It was over now. She had completed her testimony and made
her last trip down to the courthouse. Never again would Cimine
have to face her father. Several more witnesses, including her
brother, would take the stand. In the end, after hearing both
his children testify against him, Stephen would stun the court
by interrupting his trial to plead guilty. The judge would sentence him to ten to twenty years in prison.

Now, the girl sat silently, staring out the window, refusing
to engage in even casual conversation with Carolann.

The car pulled up to the school where Cimine's foster mother
was waiting for her, and Carolann tried to make amends. "I
know you've been through a rough time, Cimine, but I'm sure
everything will be all right now."

The girl ignored her, continuing to look away.

"You have a lot to look forward to. You have nice foster
parents and new friends and a new home. And we'll do everything in our power to see that your father . . ."

Before Carolann could even finish the sentence, Cimine had
shoved the car door open. She turned to look at Carolann one
last time, a look that seethed with pain and anger and seemed
to say, "You used me and now you are throwing me away
because you really don't care about me."

And it hurt.

She had longed for the impossible, the hugs and the kisses
of a grateful young girl, the tearful good-bye. But what was
happening was just the opposite. Sitting in the car now, Carolann knew that Cimine herself felt that testifying had been the
right thing to do. The sad part was that she had come to despise
Carolann for being the person to make her do it.

Carolann tried one last time, touching Cimine softly on the
arm, but the girl brushed her hand off. Then, without a word
of farewell, she stepped to the pavement, slammed the car door

as hard as she could and walked out of Carolann Natale's life forever.

Detectives usually don't wear their emotions on their sleeves. Baring one's innermost feelings while on the job is considered unprofessional conduct, a sign of weakness in the eyes of one's peers, and most detectives have mastered the art of maintaining that no-nonsense, thick-skinned veneer. But sometimes it's really no more than an act. For deep inside, under those tough exteriors, there are some things—the murder of a child, the rape of a young girl, the beating of an elderly widow—that do get to them. Touch them. Leave them feeling whipped.

And, on the day she said good-bye to Cimine, Detective Carolann Natale might have admitted that there are even a few things that make them want to cry.

CHAPTER FOUR

Carolann's first case in Manhattan was open and shut. A grounder, as the guys in the squad might say.

"You caught one," said Ty Harrison, the civilian aide in the office, just as she walked into the Fourth Homicide Zone, her new command, one chilly morning in February of 1978.

"Oh yeah?" said Carolann. "Where?"

"One-seven-five east one hundred tenth street, apartment twelve E for Edward."

"Who's over there?"

"They got the night watch team."

"Whaddya know about it?"

"All I know is some woman got shot in the kitchen. They got a guy in custody."

Driving over by herself in a squad car, Carolann was ap-

prehensive. She already had had a taste of homicide, up in the
Bronx, but this was her first case in the big city. The curtain
raiser in a new squad. The male detectives would be all eyes
and ears, waiting for some slip-up, some mistake. Women on
the job were always under a magnifying glass, compelled to
prove themselves again and again. Don't screw it up now, she
thought.

Things to remember: Get to the scene before the body is
disturbed, then compose a mental picture of how the murder
went down. Pinpoint the trajectory of the bullet, where the
gunman was standing. Try to recover all the available evidence—the weapon, the bullets, the shell casings, the bloody
clothing. Round up all the witnesses and bring them back to
the stationhouse for questioning.

The building was a ratty-looking tenement in Spanish Harlem, landscaped with great heaps of garbage. Garbage in metal
cans, garbage in black plastic bags, garbage lying loose, cas-
cading from the sidewalk into the street. Beer cans and grape-
fruit skins and chicken gizzards and empty Ripple bottles and
eggshells. On either side of the entrance there were bodegas
and shops with accordion-like iron gratings stretched across
their windows, making them look like prison cells. The front
door of number 175 was adorned with spray-painted graffiti.
"Alex," said the one that was lettered vertically, down the side
of the frame.

Carolann walked inside, into a hallway that reeked of urine
and was illuminated by a bare lightbulb in the ceiling with a
pull-cord attached. The walls were pockmarked and ugly. Huge
chunks of plaster had been gouged from the sides, and cracks
in the paint branched off in a dozen different directions, like
giant spiderwebs.

On the fourth floor a crowd was milling. Wall-to-wall cops
and detectives, some on the landing, others drifting in and out
of an apartment. For some reason, the door to the apartment
had been removed from its hinges. "Damn!" thought Carolann,
figuring that with all the human traffic either the body had been
moved or a piece of furniture dislodged or a fingerprint obliterated. Such disruptions were accidental and commonplace,
but they would make it all the more difficult for her to do her

job and to mentally reconstruct the scene of the crime at the moment it was committed.

A beefy patrolman blocked the entrance to the apartment and waved Carolann off. Probably thought she was another friend or relative of the deceased. Carolann pulled her gold shield from her purse.

"I'm Detective Natale from Fourth Homicide. You the first uniformed officer on the scene?"

The cop backed off, nonplused. "No, no...he was," he said, pointing to another officer who was standing in the apartment foyer.

The cop in the hallway looked shaken. He brushed a hand across his forehead, which was beaded with perspiration.

"I'm Detective Natale from Fourth Homicide. What happened?"

He shook his head. "That son-of-a-bitch came close to getting his head blown off, that's what happened! As we come in, he's standing there in the kitchen, leaning up against the wall like a zombie. His right hand is down by his side and the gun is in his hand. He sees me, he starts to raise his hand, all the time just lookin' at me. He's lucky I didn't blow him away. I grab the hand, twist it behind his back, and take the gun away. Then he hands me three live rounds he's holding in his other hand. And all the time, he just keeps mumbling, 'I didn't mean to kill her, I didn't mean to kill her, it was an accident...'"

"How'd you get the call?"

"Job came over the radio at about oh-six-five-oh hours as 'shots fired.' My partner and I pull up just as another sector car gets to the scene. We all go into the building together. We get as far as the second floor when this Doberman pinscher comes running out, snarling at us. Then some guy comes running down the steps and calls the dog off. The boyfriend of the deceased. He says he's the one who called 911. Tells us there's been a shooting in apartment twelve E."

"Where's the suspect now?" asked Carolann.

"Squad car took him over to the two-three precinct."

"Got a name on him?"

The officer glanced at his notepad. "Juan Rodriguez. That's

his sister-in-law in there he blew away."

"Where are the witnesses?"

"In the living room," said another uniformed cop, who was standing nearby.

"Got their names?"

He tore a piece of paper from his notepad and handed it over. Carolann started toward the kitchen, but found the way blocked by half a dozen weeping neighbors assembled at the end of the hall. She turned back toward the cop who had handed her the paper.

"Officer, would you please remove everyone from the premises who was not at the scene of the homicide? And keep them out." When the evacuation had ended, Carolann entered the kitchen.

The victim was seated at an oval table, slumped across the red-and-orange plastic tablecloth. Her head was turned sideways and it rested on her left shoulder, just inches from a salt shaker that had toppled over. Her left hand dangled limply over the edge of the table. The fingernails looked as though they had just been manicured and dabbed with a fresh coat of ruby-colored polish. She wore a pink, white and green sleeveless nightgown, and her other hand rested demurely in her lap.

She was a young Hispanic woman, short and pudgy, but with a smooth-skinned, pretty face and a full head of long, dark hair. Her eyes and mouth were closed and, oddly enough, her expression was serene. If not for the bullet hole in her thorax and the faint smudge of blood on her nightgown, she could have been napping.

The most startling thing, though, was not the corpse, but the wall hanging directly behind it. An enormous woven tapestry, four feet high and six feet long, done in vivid maroons, blues, reds, and golds: Christ, seated at the center of a long banquet table, surrounded by a dozen wide-eyed Apostles. It was a garish reproduction of the *Last Supper*, a fitting backdrop for the dead woman at the table below.

The whole scene was macabre, somebody's idea of a bad joke. Across the room, two cheap ceramic masks hung from a wall, taking in the tableau with idiotic grins.

There were four witnesses waiting in the living room—one

frail old lady, one young woman sitting on a fold-out cot, and two young men standing off to the sides. One of the men casually pulled an afro pick from the back pocket of his jeans and started to tease his hair, a gesture of indifference that made Carolann despise him instantly.

"I'm Detective Natale from the Fourth Homicide Zone," she announced to the four. "I'm investigating the death of Milagros Rodriguez and I want an opportunity to speak to each of you, privately. The officer here is going to take you to the precinct, so please go with him now." The four nodded, but said nothing.

As the witnesses filed out, the medical examiner trudged in, carrying a clipboard under his arm. He was an older man with receding gray hair, horn-rimmed glasses, a khaki jacket, and khaki slacks. It must have been a grueling night at the morgue, for he was tieless and his shirt collar was open. He looked exhausted.

After donning a pair of plastic gloves, he began to examine the body, touching the chalk-white skin ever so gingerly. He gently raised the head from its resting position, then placed it back down again. He brushed aside the bodice of the nightgown to get a better look at the entrance wound. Then he pushed the head forward, searching for an exit wound. There was none.

"Can you tell me the cause of death?" asked Carolann.

"Looks like one shot, just below the throat," said the M.E. An autopsy would later determine that the bullet had penetrated the chest cavity and severed both the aorta and the spinal cord.

Two plainclothesmen from the crime scene unit walked in just as Carolann started to sketch a diagram of the floor plan with her pen. From large, leather-bound cases, the forensic experts pulled out their instruments and flash cameras. One started to snap pictures of the body, the kitchen, the hallway, and the entrance to the apartment.

"Need anything dusted?" asked the other.

"Why don't you do the table?" suggested Carolann. "We got a weapon at the precinct. That needs dusting, too."

"All right. We'll get our shots here, and then we'll head over there."

Just before leaving, Carolann turned to the two uniformed

cops who would stay behind to stand watch over the corpse. "The morgue wagon is on the way," she said.

When Carolann walked into the squad room of the Twenty-third Precinct, the killer was sitting in a detention pen, bleary-eyed and dazed. Five-foot-six, 150 pounds, olive-smooth skin, close-cropped black hair, high cheekbones, and slanted eyes, almost Oriental-looking. Over and over again, he moaned: "Oh, my God, why did this happen? Why did this happen? I didn't mean for this to happen."

Carolann stepped up to the cell door, crooked a finger, and motioned Juan Rodriguez to step forward. He staggered closer, reeking of booze.

"C'mere, Juan. I'm Detective Natale. I'm gonna talk to you in a little while. You just sit tight for a bit, okay?" Juan nodded numbly, then stumbled back to his bench.

"Silly fuck was playing Russian roulette," muttered one of the other detectives in the office. "He didn't think it would go off—but, surprise, it did." The gun, a silver-plated .32-caliber Smith and Wesson revolver with white adhesive tape wrapped around the handle, was resting now on top of a metal desk. One of the forensic men stepped up and took a picture.

The four witnesses had been waiting on a bench near the entrance to the office when Carolann came in. One by one, she interviewed them, and each gave the same story. They had all been out late together the night before, listening to music at a local social club and drinking heavily. When they returned to the apartment, Juan began horsing around with the revolver, spinning the chamber, dry firing at the walls, pointing the gun at the others. "Click . . . click . . . bang," and Milagros, his sister-in-law, fell dead. It was an accident, they insisted. He didn't mean to do it.

"What was said in the kitchen?" Carolann asked Roman, the young man who had annoyed her by tending to his coiffure while everyone else in the apartment was trying to come to grips with a murder.

"Hey, man, I can't tell you what was said." Roman had moved to her desk and was slumped in the chair alongside.

She repeated the question, more sharply this time, enunciating the words very slowly: "I said...I want...to know...exactly...what...was said. Understand?"

Roman sat up, like an obedient pup. "I said, 'Christ man, put the fucking gun away. You wanna kill somebody?'"

Suddenly, without any warning, a middle-aged Hispanic woman sprinted into the squad room, right past the detectives and up to the cell where Juan was imprisoned.

"Ay Dios!" she bellowed. "My Juan! Ay Dios! Ay Dios!" The woman—Juan's mother—promptly fainted, collapsing on the floor. Several detectives rushed to her side. One ran for a cup of water. But Carolann, accustomed to such melodramatic outbursts by the relatives of suspects who were thrown into jail, simply continued with her interview.

Not unexpectedly, the mother made a full and rapid recovery, and she was quickly escorted from the squad office by the other detectives. The four witnesses were ushered into another room and told to wait. Carolann unlocked the door of Juan's cell and sat him down by her desk.

"Coffee?" she asked.

"Yeah."

She went to the Mister Coffee machine in the other room and brought some back in a styrofoam cup with milk and sugar.

"Comfortable?"

"Yeah, I'm okay." Juan sat with his palms down, head bowed, a paragon of remorse.

"Wanna smoke?"

"No."

"You understand English okay?"

"A little bit."

Carolann asked one of the Spanish-speaking uniformed officers to act as interpreter. She handed the officer a small, printed card and he translated the words into Spanish, advising Juan of his rights. The cop then asked Juan if he understood and would agree to speak to them without a lawyer being present. Wearily, Juan nodded yes.

"Don't nod," interjected Carolann. "Answer yes or no."

"Yes."

Then, speaking through the interpreter, Carolann began:
"Now, Juan, in your own words, I want you to tell me

exactly what happened. Where were you earlier last evening?"

"I was at the club, playing in the band. I play the horn."

"Where's the club?"

"One hundred and fifth street."

"What time did you finish?"

"I don't know exactly, but it was late. Then I went to my cousin's house."

"Where's that?"

"One seventy-five east one hundred tenth street."

"Who was there when you got there?"

"My sister-in-law, Milagros. Roman, Maria, Jose and Elena."

"What did you do when you got there?"

"Drink beer and talk, that's all, just talk."

"Then what happened?"

"I took out the gun and put it on top of the table. She got nervous. She took it from the table and put it on top of the refrigerator."

"Who put the gun on top of the refrigerator?"

"Milagros, my sister-in-law."

"Where did this gun come from?"

"It was my gun. I bought it three weeks ago."

"What kind of gun was it?"

"A thirty-two."

"Where'd you get it?"

"I bought it from some guy on First Avenue, I don't know his name. I paid twenty-five dollars for it."

"Why did you need a gun, Juan?"

"I'm a super in my building. I have to go down to the basement sometimes. But there are no doors in front or back. It's got a wall, that's all. Nothing covering the outside. You got to walk out there where the boiler room is. I need the gun for protection."

"Were you carrying the weapon with you all last night?"

"Yes."

"Was it loaded?"

"I always carry it without the cartridges in it. I had it unloaded. I had the cartridges separate."

Juan leaned over the desk to sip from his coffee. His hand was trembling too much to lift the cup to his mouth.

"Tell me again," Carolann continued, "what happened in the kitchen?"

"I took the gun out and put it on the table. Milagros got scared, so she took it and put it on top of the refrigerator."

"Then?"

"She kept talking about it, asking me why I had the gun. I took out a cartridge and put it in the gun. Then, I put the gun back on the table."

"Go on."

"I started showing off, pointing at her, pointing at the walls."

"What was Milagros doing?"

His voice began to quiver and his eyes grew moist.

"She was begging me to stop, to put the gun down. I took one cartridge and put it in one of the chambers. I counted four and started clicking the gun. I don't remember how many times, two, three, I think. I thought there was another click left, but when I pulled the trigger, it just went off. Oh, God, I didn't mean this to happen! I didn't mean to kill her! I didn't—"

Carolann cut him off. "How much did you have to drink last night, Juan?"

"About ten, eleven drinks, that's all."

"How many would you say again?"

"Maybe fourteen, fifteen drinks. I was mixing liquor with beer. Got to be way over fifteen, I guess. I don't know how many beers."

"Shot glasses, too?"

"Two-inch glasses, yeah. Glass filled to about half, and twelve-ounce bottles of Miller beer."

"Juan, at the time you took the weapon out, you knew it was a weapon?"

"Yeah, I knew."

"You knew what you were doing, is that correct?"

"I knew, I knew it was dangerous to play with that gun."

"You ignored the danger, is that correct?"

"Yes, but who could have known that was going to happen? I didn't mean to kill her. Who could have known?"

Pathetic, stupid man, Carolann thought to herself, you should have known. God, how little a life was worth to some people! But despite her contempt for the man in front of her, she kept her thoughts to herself and showed no expression. She was a professional and she had a job to do and no matter how much she personally loathed a suspect, it would simply not do to betray her feelings in front of him or the other detectives.

Carolann finished jotting the notes of her interview in a spiral pad. Juan seemed relieved that it was over, exorcised of some demon that had haunted him. "Juan," said Carolann, "you're going to have to tell this story one more time."

Juan looked up at her. "To who?"

"To the assistant district attorney. He's on his way over right now."

Carolann locked him back into his cell. "You want another coffee before he comes?" she asked.

"No," said Juan, and he slumped back toward his bench.

Juan Rodriguez was charged with murder and the Russian roulette case was officially closed. But on the next tour of duty, the detectives of the Fourth Homicide Zone gave Carolann the business.

"Congratulations," shouted one. "You broke the ice. First collar with the squad."

"Yeah," replied Carolann, "but it was an easy one. A ground ball."

"Stick around, Natale," snorted one of the other detectives. "We'll be catching plenty of others."

There were, indeed, plenty of other cases to come along in Fourth Homicide. Each would be assigned to a particular detective. That detective would have responsibility for directing the investigation, making the arrest when the time came, and taking the case to court. In the jargon of the job, the detective assigned the case was the detective who was "catching." It was another extension of the homicide baseball metaphor, the same one which transformed easy cases into "ground balls," cases involving two bodies at one scene into "doubles" and successful searches and raiding parties into "home runs."

Even though one detective might be catching, the other detectives in the squad were always ready to lend a hand. And whenever a fresh homicide or suicide was reported, all the detectives who were available would "roll," jumping into their cars and speeding straight to the scene.

Over the next four months, Carolann visited one gruesome scene after another. There was the Columbia University student who was so distraught over his grades that he leaped off the top of a building and smashed himself into a hundred pieces in the courtyard below. And the middle-aged homosexual who was stabbed and slashed to death in his East Side apartment. And a lonely old man who hung himself by tossing a rope over the door and jumping off a chair, dangling blue-faced and bug-eyed until the police cut him down. And a seventy-eight-year-old barfly whose head was bashed in by one of the young boys he liked to pick up and bring home. Carolann saw them all, steeling herself not to look away. The body was no longer a human being, she would tell herself, but a piece of a puzzle. It was her job to help solve that puzzle, coolly, methodically, and without hysteria.

Among the male detectives, there was always an unspoken but lingering fear about women cops wilting in moments of danger. A dark hallway . . . a male cop gets jammed up . . . some guy pulls a gun and the only other cop around is a female. Is she gonna go for her gun? Is she gonna freeze up? Or is she gonna hightail it out of there?

One day, up in the Bronx, Carolann and two male detectives and a sergeant were cruising around looking for two suspects in a murder case. The car stopped at a grocery store and two of the detectives walked inside to have a look around. Carolann stayed behind in the back seat with an eyewitness to the crime. Sgt. Bill Taylor sat in the front seat, behind the steering wheel. Suddenly, the eyewitness whispered: "Hey, I think that's them standing across the street!"

Taylor didn't delay for a moment. "Let's take 'em!" he barked.

He hit the accelerator, swung the car around, then screeched to a halt at an odd angle across the pavement. Yanking a revolver from his hip holster, he pushed open the left front door, jumped down beside it, and shouted: "Freeze! Police! Up against the wall!"

Taylor looked back to find Carolann right beside him,

crouching behind the rear door and training her gun directly at the two suspects. He nodded to her, and they stepped out cautiously from behind the car, moving toward the two men against the wall.

As Taylor began to pat one of the men down for concealed weapons, Carolann kept the other covered. The suspect kept glancing back over his shoulder, not quite believing that some "crazy broad" had gotten the drop on him.

"Put your hands up and grab ahold of that metal grating!" snapped Carolann, and the guy with the wandering eyes went rigid. "I wanna see those hands, understand? Don't move, buster, because my hand's shaking. And this gun in my hand is just liable to go off."

"Okay, lady!" answered the suspect, his knees starting to shake. "Don't shoot! I won't move. I promise, lady, I won't move. Just don't shoot!"

Later that day, after the two suspects had been hauled back to the office for questioning, the other detectives were all ears. "Heard you and Carolann had a little action up in the Bronx today," one of the men said to Taylor. "How'd she do?"

Without a moment's hesitation, Taylor replied: "She was right behind me, every step of the way. She can work with me any time."

CHAPTER FIVE

One balmy night in June, 1978, George was sprawled on his back underneath the chassis of his white 1965 Dodge, trying to figure out what to do next with the brakes. He had been working on them all afternoon, but it was just about hopeless. They were nearly shot, and he didn't have enough money to buy new ones.

"Hey, man, what's happenin'?"

George peeked out from under the car to see Lorenzo leaning against a building and gnawing on a toothpick. Henry was with him, wearing those funny-looking eyeglasses with the lenses so thick they looked like the bottoms of Coke bottles.

"Shit, man," muttered George. "I need new brakes, but ain't nobody around here gonna lend me the money to buy them. I been askin' people all afternoon."

"You wanna make some money, man?" asked Lorenzo, a peculiar gleam in his eyes.

"What do you got in mind?"

"A job."

"What kinda job?"

"Just a job, man, a job. Don't worry about it. Don't be askin' so many questions. Ain't no need to worry."

"How much is in it for me?"

"Enough, man, enough. I just got to check a few things out first. Meet us back here at eight o'clock."

Lorenzo turned and headed down the block with Henry.

George assumed they were talking about a stickup, but he realized that it might be wiser not to press Lorenzo for too many details. Lorenzo was an ex-Marine, a little crazy in the head sometimes, and it didn't pay to get him angry. After doing all he could with the brakes, George went upstairs to his apartment to wash the grease off his hands and face and change his clothes.

A couple of hours later, he returned to the street to find Lorenzo and Henry waiting for him. With them were Denny and Felix, two other guys he recognized from the block.

"They're comin' with us," said Lorenzo, and all five piled into George's Dodge.

They drove to a seedy hotel on West Ninety-third Street, where Lorenzo walked inside to buy a bag of marijuana for five dollars. Back inside the car, they rolled joints and noisily sucked down the sweet, heady smoke.

"Shee-eet!" muttered Lorenzo, stretching the word into several syllables for effect. He voiced what they all felt, for all of them had the same complaint: they were broke.

Finally, Henry got down to business. "I know this supermarket down on Amsterdam Avenue," he began. "Friend of mine works there, and he almost got me a job there, too. They must keep eight thousand dollars in that place. They got a lot of customers, people comin' and goin' all the time. Maybe you do your shoppin' and you spend fifty dollars and all that money adds up, man."

The others agreed that the supermarket would make a good target. "Start the car, George," ordered Lorenzo. Then he spelled out the plan of attack.

"We just goin' to go in and stick it up. Nobody moves, we take the money, and then we leave. We tell the people this is a stickup and we freeze the people, and then we tell the manager to open the safe box up and get the money out. Then we come out of the supermarket and get in the car."

Lorenzo pulled a .22-caliber Luger from his waistband and started to hand it to Henry. "Hey, man, could you do this gun and freeze the people?"

But Henry held up his palms to fend off the weapon. "No, man, no way. I'm on probation. I don't want nothin' to do with no guns. I don't even want to go inside."

"All right," said Lorenzo, "you just stay outside with Felix and be the lookouts. Me and Denny will do the guns." He handed the Luger to Denny.

Denny would go in with Lorenzo, even wield the gun. But he had no intention of shooting it. In fact, he wasn't even going to put any bullets in the chamber.

George would be the driver, which suited him just fine. As long as he didn't have to go inside and as long as he didn't have to carry a gun. And he might even come out of this with a couple of hundred for himself, maybe even enough to fix those damned brakes.

"Nothin's going to go wrong, man," Lorenzo reassured them. He puffed on the dying nub of a joint as the car neared its destination. "Nobody moves, nobody gets hurt, we take the money and leave."

At Amsterdam Avenue and Seventy-sixth Street, they passed the supermarket, and George made a quick U-turn. He headed east on Seventy-sixth Street, pulling to a stop twenty-five yards from the corner. The others got out and walked back toward the supermarket.

George sat in the car and waited, tapping his fingers on the steering wheel. Minutes passed, and he started to grow nervous.

Suddenly, a shot rang out.

George jerked his head around, but there was little he could see.

Felix was the first to come running around the corner. "Start it up! Start it up!" he shouted at George. Then he turned on his heels and sprinted back toward the supermarket.

Two more shots exploded.

This time, they all came racing around the corner. Denny jumped into the back seat, but the others sprinted right past the car. Lorenzo was carrying a gun in one hand and a brown paper bag in the other and trying to peel off his blue sweater, all at the same time.

"Catch up to them, man, catch up!" Denny screamed in George's ear.

George pulled alongside of Lorenzo, and Lorenzo vaulted into the front seat. "Keep on going!" Lorenzo ordered. Henry and Felix dashed off in another direction and flagged down a cab.

As the getaway car sped north, Lorenzo panted wildly, trying to control his breathing. "There was a fucking dude in the place who was packing a gun," he gasped. "I told him not to do it. I told him three times. But he went for it, moved, so I put him away. It was either him or me. He was on the floor, so I went over to him and took his gun." Lorenzo pulled a revolver out of his pants and stared at it blankly, like it was some object that had just fallen from outer space.

"What about the money, man?" asked George.

Lorenzo turned the brown paper bag upside down and the paper bills came fluttering out, landing in his lap. He counted the money. It added up to $381.

"Shit," he muttered. "To kill some dude, all for $381 . . ."

George was handed his share, a measly three tens and one five. That might pay for a few beers and a little smoke, maybe even a meal at that Chinese-Cuban joint that he liked. But it certainly wouldn't buy him a new set of brakes.

And already, off in the distance, the police sirens were beginning to wail.

"Italian tonight, Carolann?"

"How about Chinatown? I could go for a little Szechuan."

"Nah, we had Chinese last night. I'm up to my eyeballs in egg rolls. What about some pasta with clam sauce? We could hit that place that you like down in Little Italy."

"Too fattening. I'm trying to lose a couple of pounds."

"Might as well go to the Greeks for a burger, then. Anyway, it's near the office."

"Some gourmet you are, John. Cops have no imagination."

Carolann Natale and John Quealy were driving back from an interview on one of John's cases, wrestling with a decision about where to dine that night, when the radio in their car crackled to life:

"Units in the vicinity of two-two-three Amsterdam Avenue . . . Report of a man shot . . . Ten-twenty . . . in a supermarket."

"Uh oh, better forget about that dinner for a while," said Carolann. "If that guy goes DOA, it's my case."

"On the way," said John, a tall, graying, bespectacled man who looked more like a Presbyterian minister than a New York City homicide detective. He nudged the accelerator to the floor and headed west through Central Park.

Three minutes later, the detectives pulled up to the supermarket. A crowd of gawkers and curiosity-seekers stood outside, craning their necks to peer into the plate-glass windows. A dozen squad cars were parked in front, some right up on the sidewalk. The first officers on the scene already had roped off the entrance with red tape, stretching it from the door to two parking meters on the curb to form a rectangle.

Carolann Natale walked briskly toward the entrance, nodding to some of the other detectives. No second guessing this time. She had worked homicide for more than six months now, and she knew exactly what she had to do.

A uniformed cop was standing just inside the door.

"Whatta we got?" asked Carolann.

"A stickup," said the officer. "You got one dead inside the store, one shot out on the street. Guy on the street is at the hospital now, in good condition. Just a graze, and they recovered the bullet. One of your detectives is over there now doing an interview. Hispanic kid outside got a plate number on the car. They're doing a check on it now."

The supermarket was only a few blocks away from the offices of the Fourth Homicide Zone, so other detectives had been on the scene within minutes of the shootings. They had questioned some of the witnesses, come up with a description of the getaway car and returned to the office to do a computer check on the license plate.

Carolann walked past the checkout counters, toward the rear of the store. The first thing she noticed was a large puddle of blood in the center of the floor. Curiously, the corpse was lying at least four feet away from the puddle. She looked more closely and noticed bands of blood, stretching across the floor from the puddle toward the body. Puddle in one spot, body in another, drag marks in between. Clearly, the victim had been moved after he was shot, probably to conceal him from view through the front windows.

The body lay in one of the aisles, covered by a white sheet. On the shelves around it were stacks of bottled mouthwash, cans of creamed corn, jars of pickles, containers of fruit juice and boxes of disposable trash bags. Two feet jutted out from the bottom of the sheet, one turned to the left and the other to the right. A Hush Puppy loafer from the right foot lay stranded on the floor a short distance from the body.

As John Quealy stood behind her, snapping pictures with his Polaroid, Carolann kneeled and pulled the top of the sheet back from the corpse.

The victim, a white male, looked to be about sixty years old. His head was turned to the left side, resting in still another puddle of blood that had congealed into a sticky red halo on the floor. The right eye had been shot out and the entire right side of the face was awash with blood. A pair of eyeglasses still rested in position on the man's head. The bullet apparently had shattered the right lens, penetrated the right eye, and lodged in the brain. Carolann glanced up at the cash register from where the shot had been fired, then back down at the body, measuring what appeared to be a considerable distance in her mind. Whoever had pulled the trigger, she decided, must have been one hell of a shot.

She studied the body again, and her eyes drifted to the black leather holster clipped to the front of the dead man's belt. The holster was empty and it rested at an awkward angle, flipped from the inside of the trousers to the outside. The dead man obviously had been carrying a gun, but it looked like someone had searched him and removed it.

"Hey, John," said Carolann, walking back toward the cash registers. "Any word on who our victim was?"

"Yeah," answered John. "Looks like we got a heavy one this time."

The dead man, Bob Parker, had owned a men's clothing shop a block away and lived just around the corner. He had been licensed to wear a pistol because he often carried large amounts of cash from his shop to the bank. Apparently, he had been inside the supermarket doing some shopping when the holdup men burst through the front door. Parker had broken up stickups before, and he tried to play the Good Samaritan once again. This time, one of the gunmen was too quick for him.

A community leader and an active member of virtually all the major civic groups, Parker had been known to be a friend of the police. Many of the police commanders and detectives knew him on a first-name basis. The word was already out that they felt a personal obligation to find his murderer—and find him fast.

The checkout counters were still covered with bulky brown bags, some lying on their sides with groceries tumbling out. Once the shooting had started, the customers had left their purchases to dash for cover. Carolann walked up to the store manager, a short, stocky man of about fifty who was wearing a suit and tie.

"Excuse me," she began, "I'm Detective Natale."

"I'll help you in any way I can," he sputtered, "anything you want . . . it could have been me . . . anything you want . . . anything." Still trembling with shock, the manager kept repeating himself, like a broken record.

"Calm down, calm down," said Carolann. "Now, just start from the beginning and tell me what happened."

"But I already told the other detectives . . . told them everything . . . anything I can do to help . . ."

"Well, tell me," said Carolann. "I'm gonna be responsible for this case. So take a minute to relax, then just start again from the beginning."

The manager took a deep breath, then exhaled slowly.

"I had just shut off the automatic doors because it was getting near closing time," he began. "People had to push the doors open to get out. One of the customers was leaving. When she pushed open the door, a guy squeezed in from the outside. I don't know where he came from. The next thing I know, there's a gun at my head. The guy is saying, 'All your money, I want all your money.'

"I said, 'I don't have any money.' I was standing talking to the security guard, so he made both of us lie down on the floor, face down. Then he went through our pockets and took our wallets. He told us, 'Don't move or I'll kill you.' He kept saying it over and over, 'Don't move, keep your head down, don't look back at me or I'll kill you. I'm a pro, I know what I'm doing.' We were afraid to move. We couldn't see anything. The next thing I know, I hear a shot."

Carolann interrupted his narrative. "How much time had elapsed?"

"To me, it seemed like an eternity," replied the manager. "I know it was just a short time, less than a minute at most."

"Was the man who fired the shot the same man who held the gun on you?"

"I don't know. I couldn't see him. I wasn't going to move; he would have shot me. I really can't tell you anything more . . . people were running and screaming, all kinds of commotion. I stayed down until my cashier came over and said, 'They're gone.'"

"Which of the employees are still in the store?" asked Carolann.

"Elena's here," said the manager, pointing to a pretty, dark-haired Hispanic girl who was standing in front of the frozen vegetable counter. Elena had put a jacket on, over her work uniform, and slung her pocketbook over her shoulder. She was obviously preparing to leave, so Carolann moved quickly to intercept her.

"I don't want to get involved," the girl protested, trying to shake Carolann off. "They'll kill me. They know what I look like. This is a dangerous job. I'm gonna quit this place, I've had it."

Carolann persisted. "Listen, Elena, no one is going to force you to do what you don't want to do. Whatever you tell us will be strictly between you and me. But whatever you tell us could be extremely important. It could help us find these people. Think about that for a second."

Finally, Elena relented. "All right, Detective, I'll tell you, but I'm not gonna tell anybody else. This is the last time I'm gonna tell anybody anything."

"Start from the beginning," said Carolann, a deliberate tone of reassurance to her voice.

"I was working cash register number one," said Elena. She pointed. "The one nearest the door. That's the express checkout. I couldn't believe my eyes. I turned, and there's a guy standing there, pointing a gun at me, with his finger on the trigger. I couldn't believe what I was seeing. I even asked him, 'Are you kidding?' He said, 'Yeah, that's right, I'm kidding, I'm kidding.' He just kept standing there, staring at me, with a gun in his hand. Then I heard another man say, 'Nobody move, everybody on the floor and nobody will get hurt.' And then the man next to me said, 'That's right, no one move and no one will get killed.'"

"Where was the other man standing?" asked Carolann.

"In front of the third and fourth registers, near the window."

"Did you see him?"

"I could see he had a gun, but I couldn't see him well enough to describe him."

"He say anything else?"

"He yelled something like, 'Don't try it! Drop it!' Maybe both, I'm not sure. I knew he was talking to a customer. Then I heard a shot."

"What happened next?"

"The man that did the shooting said, 'Put the money in the bag.' He was talking to the girls. The man near me said, 'Put the money in the bag.' At first, I didn't. I told him to do it himself. But then he grabbed my arm and he put the gun at my back, so I did what he said."

"What happened next?"

"The man near me said, 'Nobody move for five minutes or you'll get killed.' Then he walked out the door. The other man—the man who did the shooting—walked out after him, walking backwards."

As Carolann jotted notes in a pad, Elena provided a description of the man who had pulled a gun on her and forced her to empty the register: Hispanic, early twenties, five-foot-eight, 150 pounds, medium complexion, small scars around the cheeks, curly afro, long-sleeved black shirt, dark pants, spoke Spanish with an unusual accent, possibly Dominican. It was a good description, remarkably detailed—right down to the silver filling in the upper left side of the gunman's mouth and the gold wire stretched across his upper front teeth.

By the time Carolann and John Quealy returned to the office, some two hours later, it looked like the detectives were bracing for an invasion. Some were strapping extra revolvers to their waists. Others were checking the holsters above their ankles. One walked by carrying a sleek, black shotgun. A posse was forming. The hunt was on.

"What's goin' on?" asked Carolann. "Somebody get a hit on that license plate?"

"We got a name and an address," answered one of the detectives. "We're going up there now to see if we can take him."

Four detectives started for the stairs. Carolann checked her own holster, then made a move to join them. But she was cut off at the door by one of the bosses.

"Natale, you stay here. We got enough people going. We need you to coordinate all the information on the case."

The posse headed out, and Carolann walked back to a desk. For a few moments, she busied herself studying the notes left behind by the other detectives who had interviewed witnesses at the scene. Then she glanced at the computer read-out from the Department of Motor Vehicles on the license plate check. The telephone rang, and she deftly put off an inquisitive news-paper reporter with the usual disclaimer: "Sorry, but I have no further information on the homicide at this time. All the de-tectives are out in the field."

By all appearances, she was cool and calm, a model of efficiency and composure. But in her gut, she was ready to scream.

They had brushed her off and left her behind, explanations aside. No matter that it was officially her case. It was the same old bugaboo about women cops in dangerous situations. Regardless of how often they proved themselves, when the going got rough, most men just didn't want them around. The boss might have given her some song and dance about coordinating the information, but his real message was all too clear: Don't get in the way, little girl.

She had heard it before. "We're not gonna take a woman along if we have to break down a door," many of the detectives would insist. Yet they didn't seem to have an answer when Carolann would shoot back: "Well, maybe if you took a woman along, you wouldn't have to break down the door in the first place!"

Carolann was still smarting from the snub when the posse returned, forty minutes later, with a suspect in tow. He was a tall, thin Dominican with a scraggly afro, a stubble of beard on his chin and a sleepy, vacant look in his eyes. His hands were cuffed securely behind him.

"Inside," said one of the detectives, nudging the prisoner into a private room. "Sit down." The detective closed the door.

They would wait at least twenty minutes to a half hour before beginning the interrogation. For the detectives, it was a time to unwind, come down emotionally after the raid, have a cup of coffee and swap fresh tidbits of information. But it was also a deliberate ploy, designed to make their unattended prisoner sweat and squirm, wondering why it was taking so long and what in God's name was going to happen to him next.

And the more he sweated and squirmed, the more likely it was that George, the hapless driver of that white Dodge with the shoddy brakes, would tell the detectives exactly what they wanted to know about the murder.

"When was the first time that you learned that somebody had been killed?"

"Lorenzo was saying that the man was moving when he walked in and he said stickup, please nobody move, and while they were getting ready to take the money, he said someone went for it."

"Meaning a gun?"

"Yes. So when he saw that the person went for it, he had no other choice."

"So he was kind of forced to shoot because he went for his gun?"

"Yes."

"How do you feel about that?"

"Personally, it feels like a nightmare."

Once they had started the interrogation, George cracked like an eggshell. Names, addresses, the plan to rip off the supermarket, the fact that Lorenzo had done the shooting, even his own meager cut from the heist. He gave it up, all of it. First he gave it up to the detectives who had tracked him down through the license plate on his car and arrested him just as he walked into his apartment. Then he gave it up to Carolann, who read him his rights and took a statement. Finally, he gave it up in another statement taken by the assistant district attorney, Myles Malman.

At 6:30 a.m., a second posse of detectives trudged through the door.

"You'll never guess where we found this one," said one of the detectives, shoving a handcuffed prisoner ahead of him. "Under his mother's bed. As soon as we came to the door, he tried to hide. Had to goose him out with shotguns."

The moment they marched the second suspect in, Carolann felt a twinge of recognition and a small measure of triumph, remembering how she had buttonholed the reluctant checkout girl, Elena, and badgered her into giving a statement. No question about it, they had the right man. The silver filling in the upper left side of his mouth, the gold wire stretched across his upper front teeth . . . Elena's description fit Denny, the reluctant gunman, to a tee.

Like George, Denny quickly caved in and gave the detectives a full statement, implicating himself and the others.

By 11:45 a.m., still another posse returned with a third suspect, a dark-skinned black man with a mustache and goatee, wearing eyeglasses with thick lenses. They had grabbed Henry, the myopic mastermind behind the stickup, just as he was walking into his grandmother's apartment. He, too, made a full confession.

Two other suspects remained at large, but not for long. The heat was on, and they knew it. That night Lorenzo gave himself up at the studios of WABC-TV. Detectives from the Fourth Homicide Zone arrived soon after to take him into custody. And early the following morning, a mopey-faced man in a gray wool sea captain's cap walked into the Twenty-fourth Precinct stationhouse on West One-hundredth Street. The officer on the desk looked down at him with curiosity.

"I think the police are looking for me," said Felix, the fifth and last member of the stickup team.

Forty-eight hours after the crime was committed, George, Lorenzo, Denny, Henry, and Felix were taken one by one out of separate detention pens, escorted through a heavy wood door, and marched before a judge on the first floor of Manhattan Criminal Court.

On the other side of the courtroom, Carolann Natale sat silent and sullen. She was exhausted from all the interviews, the lineups, and the paperwork. She was bleary-eyed from lack of sleep. And she was still cross with the other detectives for excluding her from their raiding parties.

The most important thing, though, was that the case had been solved. All the detectives had contributed to the investigation, and the team effort had produced stunning results.

So, putting aside the matter of individual pride for the moment, Carolann attended to the business at hand. She stood in the crowded courtroom and walked by herself down the aisle. Past the spectators, past the other cops waiting for their cases to be called, past the thieves, the hookers, and the other petty criminals. Pushing open a small gate, she approached the bench. And then she stood by as the judge arraigned the five frightened men at her side, the first step necessary to bring them to trial for Bob Parker's murder.

Not long after the supermarket stickup, Carolann had the dubious distinction of being assigned to two homicide cases in a single day. Moreover, both cases turned out to be "doubles."

The first took place in the ground-floor apartment of a tenement on the fringes of Spanish Harlem. An Oriental man, clad only in his undershorts, was found lying in the kitchen with a length of rope knotted around his neck. A young Oriental woman, tiny and doll-like, was found partially nude in the bedroom, also with a rope around her neck.

At first glance, it could have been a double suicide by hanging, some sort of ritual death perhaps. But on closer inspection, Carolann and Mike Strong, the first detective on the scene, noticed that the necks of the victims showed no vertical stretch marks, marks that would have appeared if the bodies had been dangling for some time. The ropes were imbedded deeply in the flesh, a clear indication that both victims had been garroted.

The boyfriend of the dead woman had found the bodies and notified the police. Now he sat in the living room, muttering and cursing at the detectives. "What the fuck you all doin' here?" he wanted to know. "Why don't you take the bodies out? Why the fuck you just leavin' 'em here?"

The man was high as a kite, his mind a muddle from all the cocaine he had snorted. He seemed like a logical suspect, but his alibi was iron-clad. A musician by trade, he had been playing a gig at a nightclub in full view of forty or fifty witnesses at the time the two Orientals had been murdered.

From the boyfriend and the neighbors, the detectives learned that the dead woman was a high-priced prostitute, catering strictly to Oriental men. An Oriental social club would send customers over, in exchange for a cut of her earnings. In the living room, the detectives found a thick file listing the names of hundreds of clients of the dead woman.

The medical examiner arrived and told Carolann and the other detectives that the victims might have been knocked unconscious before they were strangled. Consequently, the detectives came up with several theories about the murders. One was that the killer was an Oriental with an expert knowledge of the martial arts and had knocked both victims out with karate chops before killing them. A second theory held that the dead man was a gambler and owed money. His creditors had decided to kill him, and then they murdered the girl because she was a witness. Still a third theory was that the girl was the main target, marked for revenge because she had failed to kick back enough money on her earnings to the Oriental social club. In any case, the theories would remain theories. The case was never solved.

The second double homicide was equally intriguing. Two gunmen had finagled their way into a luxury high-rise and taken the elevator to the top floor. There, they managed to get inside the apartment of a well-known madam. They had apparently been sent to kill the madam because she had welched on a payment for a delivery of drugs. But once inside, the two assassins were surprised by the madam's boyfriend, who emerged from the bedroom with a .45-caliber handgun. The boyfriend shot both of the gunmen. One died instantly, the other in the ambulance on the way to the hospital. The madam was wounded in the arm during the shooting, but her injury was not serious.

Fresh from finishing the paperwork on the first double homicide, Carolann arrived at the scene of number two to find one of the dead gunmen still sprawled on the floor of the vestibule, a bullet hole in his back. Detectives had already found a residue of cocaine around the toilet seat in the bathroom and a glassine envelope in the trash basket nearby, indicating that somebody had done a sloppy job of disposing of the evidence. They had also discovered dozens of pornographic pictures showing the madam and her boyfriend in a variety of explicit poses.

Clearly, there was evidence in the apartment of a number of criminal acts, not to mention the shootings. Yet, in the end, nobody went to jail.

Detective Natale arrested the boyfriend and charged him with two homicides, possession of a weapon, and possession of narcotics. But when the case was presented to the grand jury, the madam testified that her boyfriend had shot the two intruders in self-defense. The weapons charge turned out to be equally shaky, because one of the uniformed police officers first on the scene had inadvertently picked up the gun, a .45-caliber automatic, and retrieved it from the bedroom, making it impossible to prove conclusively that it had been in the boyfriend's possession. Lastly, the narcotics charge was never even presented to the grand jury, because the court clerk had omitted certain crucial wording when he had typed up the search warrant. Even though the cops had found traces of cocaine and a glassine envelope, the clerk's blunder made it impossible to introduce the evidence in court.

The detectives' hands were tied. Because of a string of legal technicalities, the grand jury dismissed all charges and the boyfriend walked free.

Fate, however, sometimes takes unexpected twists in a homicide investigation. One morning, about five months later, Carolann received a call from a detective on the Lower West Side.

"Remember that guy you locked up for the double homicide in the penthouse, the one that walked?" the detective began. "Well, he's in the hospital now, breathing his last. He was sitting in a pimp bar down here last night, nursing a Scotch, when three guys come in to do a stickup. He goes for his gun, and one of them just blows him away."

And that morning, the boyfriend who had beaten the murder rap died, himself the victim of a murderer's bullets.

CHAPTER SIX

For an office preoccupied with death, the Fourth Homicide Zone on West Eighty-second Street was surprisingly brimming with life.

Detective John Barna, a compact dynamo of nervous energy, lit a cigarette and lapsed into a throaty imitation of uptown jive talk while counseling Carolann Natale, the lone woman in the squad, on the best way to flush a suspect from a Harlem hideout.

"Lissen heah, Carolann. You calls up de buildin', see, an' you tells dem, 'Lemme speak to Cholly. Dis a frien' o' his. Hello, Cholly? Dis heah is Freddy. Lissen, man, you in *big* trouble. De man got de place surrounded, y'heah? He gon' do you, Cholly. He gon' *do* you!' Phht! Cholly gon' go right out de door—and den we gon' nab 'em good!"

For ethnic balance, Barna glided into his best Greek coffee-shop accent. "Yanni! Toose cups coffee plis! Side order strim-bims, hokay sport? One pis tserry pie!" Then, without skipping a beat, Barna transformed his voice into the voice of a lisping homosexual. John Barna was the detective of a thousand accents.

Detective Terrence McLinskey, a silver-haired man with the visage of a kindly village priest, touched a match to his pipe and spoke lovingly of the joys of *bel canto* opera: "Ah, Donizetti, Bellini, Rossini . . . Hey Carol, next time you go up on a roof for a stakeout, you can take my cassettes and play a little opera while you wait for your suspect to come out." Carolann laughed.

A team of detectives headed for the door, on the way to arrest a suspect. "Hey, Tom, let's go!" shouted one.

Looking up from his desk, his eyes bulging with mock terror, Detective Tom Quinn gasped, "Are you kiddin'? That man has a gun! I got twenty-two years on the job and I'm gettin' out soon. *That man has a gun, I tell you!*" Quinn reached for his coat.

A reporter entered the office in search of a story. The detectives introduced themselves and politely shook his hand. Except for Detective Al Lopez, who slapped a pair of handcuffs on the reporter's wrists.

Nearby, Detective Mike Strong was finishing up some paperwork. He was unquestionably the most nattily dressed homicide detective in the squad—pancake-pressed beige suit, cream-colored shirt, wide tie with bright flower pattern, cream-colored leather shoes with gold buckles and a glossy spit shine.

"How's it goin', Mike?" asked another detective.

"Ugh," grimaced Strong, "it's murder."

Carolann Natale and several of the other detectives sat around a table, reminiscing about their earlier years on the force, when they investigated sex crimes cases.

"One time," said Carolann, "we had a victim whose pubic hair was shaved by a rapist with a razor blade. Just took the blade and made a white band right across the hair. So the assistant district attorney says we have to get a picture before the hair grows back—for evidence. Of course, he's not gonna send one of the men detectives to take that picture. He sends me. But I hated that assignment. All the guys in the squad kept pestering me to show them the picture!"

Even though the detectives often made light of their cases with abandon, they were not nearly as nonchalant about other people's misfortunes as it might have appeared. For Carolann, especially, working sex crimes had been a deeply disturbing and unsettling experience. How many times had she felt herself empathizing with the victim, personally experiencing the revulsion and the shame, secretly thanking God over and over again that it hadn't been her or her daughter who was raped? Cops were not supposed to get caught up personally in their cases, but when it came to sex crimes, Carolann's determination to capture the culprit often built to a fever pitch. It bothered her when she couldn't make an arrest. In fact, it bothered her more than she cared to admit.

Nevertheless, she recognized the need to joke about the job as a healthy one, a kind of safety mechanism or therapeutic release for all the tensions and strains and emotions that could eat away at the best of cops after being exposed on an almost daily basis to the vilest, most sadistic kinds of human behavior. Like the wise-cracking surgeons on *M*A*S*H*, who were always elbow-deep in blood and gore, the detectives were really very compassionate people. They needed their humor, quite simply, to maintain their sanity.

By now, Detective Dominick Bologna was well into another anecdote. "We had a guy once who raped some girl, and we knew he did it, but he refused to give us a statement," Dominick was saying. "Kept telling us he didn't know anything about it, wasn't even near the apartment. So we tell him, 'Drop your pants. We're gonna have to get a print of it.'"

"You told him *what!*" exclaimed Carolann, not quite believing her ears.

"Told him we have to get a print of it. We said the rapist left prints all over the apartment. So we tell this guy, 'Drop your pants, pull down your underpants, and stick it right up here on the ink pad so we can make a print.' Guy starts to get all nervous. Then he says, 'Hey, officer, you don't have to do that, I did it, I'll confess.'"

"Reminds me of the football player who had the letters 'J-O-E' tattooed on the most cherished part of his anatomy," chimed in Detective Sam Strelzin.

"Fellah bangs up his knee in a big game, so he has to go to the hospital. Inside the hospital, all the nurses make jokes because of his unusual tattoo. But one nurse kinda falls for the guy. After he gets out of the hospital, they decide to get married. First day back after the honeymoon, the new bride comes into work and all the other nurses start teasing her. You know, about marrying the guy with 'J-O-E' tattooed on his you-know-what.

"So the new bride turns to the other nurses and says:

"'Yeah, but you only saw part of it. There's more. It says, "Joe's Pizzeria, Massapequa Park, Long Island, N.Y.'"

The banter was interrupted by a call from Lieutenant Herman Kluge, the squad commander, who summoned Carolann and the other detectives into his private office for a briefing on the latest murder.

It was a particularly brutal slaying, one that would make the front pages of the city's newspapers for days. A brilliant woman graduate student beaten, kicked, knifed, and karate-chopped to death in the room of a male friend. The male friend, a thirty-two-year-old Japanese graduate student at Columbia University, had been living in the apartment of a married couple on the Upper East Side. After the murder, he vanished. The police pegged him as the prime suspect—the jilted lover.

Lieutenant Kluge sat at his desk, shirt collar opened, tie loosened, sleeves rolled up to the elbows. He was a fair-skinned man in his fifties, with thinning, sandy-colored hair, a strong aquiline nose and piercing, pale blue eyes. Looking weary and wise at the same time, he puffed occasionally on the nub of a cigar and peered over the tops of his bifocals at some scribbled notes on the murder. Kluge, who seemed to have a radar-like sensitivity for critical details, began reciting the facts of the case, but was halted mid-way through by a curious observation that he himself made:

"Dog didn't bark—how strange!"_

About a dozen detectives had crowded around his desk.

Carolann sat on a chair, making notes in a pad as the lieutenant spoke.

"All right," Kluge continued, "this guy is thirty-two years old, Japanese, five-foot-three—and he has a black belt in karate."

"Figures," said one of the detectives. "They always have a black belt when we gotta go find 'em and lock 'em up."

Kluge went on. "Seems this fellow receives ten thousand dollars a year in allowance from his mother back in Japan."

"So he'll stay out of the country," quipped one of the other detectives.

Kluge already had interviewed a male acquaintance of the dead girl, but the young man's demeanor did not sit well with the lieutenant's own code of conduct. "I don't know. This girl must have been a product of the new morals. The guy who was just in here—I could have thrown up when I talked to him. He's only concerned with his next date."

The lieutenant opened the floor to discussion and the questions began to fly.

"Has he got a vehicle?"

"Has he got a valid passport?"

"Has he got any friends here?"

"Should we release his picture to the press?"

"Do you think he might head back to Japan?"

"Did the children of the married couple see anything or hear anything?"

Each new question during the give-and-take produced a new line of inquiry, which, in turn, generated a new assignment for individual detectives. Some were told to find the suspect's friends in New York City and interview them. Others were told to make contact with the Japanese Consulate in Manhattan, in case the suspect attempted to return to his homeland. Kluge dispatched Carolann to interview the young daughters of the couple with whom the Japanese student had lodged. Perhaps the children saw something or heard something on their way to school that morning.

Just before the detectives went on their way, Kluge offered a warning: "Watch out, the press is busting our chops on this one. They think they know more about this case than we do.

So if you get any inquiries, just refer them to me and I'll handle it."

A latecomer rushed in, huffing and puffing. "Say, can anyone give me a hand? I got a department car down the street and it's got a flat tire."

Everyone, needless to say, had urgent business to attend to.

Kluge looked at Carolann. "Aren't you going to help him change that tire? Remember what you told me when you came here—you didn't want any special privileges just because you're a woman."

Carolann grinned. "Yeah, that's right, Lieutenant. But I don't wanna do anything the guys don't wanna do, either."

The streets of Manhattan's Upper East Side were slick from drizzle as Carolann and her partner, Freddy Cappetta, headed south toward the scene of the crime. Cappetta, a freckle-faced, boyish-looking detective with an impish wit and a rapid-fire manner of speech, was bemoaning the fact that the fugitive suspect had a black belt in karate.

"You know what, Freddy," offered Carolann. "A black belt in karate doesn't do any good against a bullet."

A bald-headed man puffing an ornate, Sherlock Holmesian pipe nervously ushered Carolann and Cappetta through the front door of the apartment where the murder had occurred. It was a rambling, high-ceilinged affair in one of the mammoth prewar buildings that still dot the Upper East Side.

The missing Japanese student had lived with the Cohens and their two young daughters for four years, in a small room just off the kitchen. The mustard-colored walls of his room were splotched with bloodstains, some as big as palm prints, others no larger than finger dabs. Around the doorknobs and frames there were smudges and swirls of black powder in Rorschach-like patterns, the handiwork of the forensic experts who had dusted for fingerprints.

The corpse already had been removed. The box spring and mattress had been yanked off the bed and flipped over. Someone had pulled all the dresser drawers out and scattered the missing student's clothes and other belongings about the room. All day long, John Quealy, Carolann's partner on the supermarket case, had been sifting through photographs, letters, identity cards, calendars, bankbooks, match covers, and gum wrappers—the flotsam and jetsam of student life.

"Forensic came back," Quealy told Carolann and Cappetta. "They ripped out the sheets and took them, looking for traces of semen."

"John, you get all the grounders," teased Cappetta. "Nice apartment, all the evidence is right here." Homicide detectives delighted in good-natured razzing, needling each other about catching easy cases, and Cappetta could not pass up the opportunity.

The dining room had been turned into a temporary command post for the police investigators. Snapshots and other memorabilia were strewn across the table top. Mugs containing cold coffee, now covered with an oily film, sat in front of each setting. A plate of mandelbread, a traditional Jewish dessert, was in the center of the table. The bald-headed man and his wife had been gracious hosts to the detectives, recognizing that they had a job to do.

Carolann turned to the husband, who was sucking furiously at his pipe. "Mr. Cohen, you have two daughters who left for school early this morning?"

"Yes," he replied, puffing even harder.

"Are they available to be interviewed?"

"No, they are not. We're keeping this from them."

"Can't we talk to your little girls?"

"No, they're not even here. They're staying with friends until this blows over. We just don't want to upset them."

"Mr. Cohen, we're trying to find out what they observed. We need to talk to them. They may have seen something, some bloody clothing, perhaps."

Mr. Cohen flipped the light switch in the dining room, trying to re-create the darkness of early morning. "You see?" he asked. "The girls would have left for school this morning without being able to see anything." Mr. Cohen was adamant.

Mrs. Cohen, a short, blonde woman with thick eyeglasses, entered the apartment, breathing heavily. She was a nervous wreck because the newspapers had quoted her by name.

"Where did the papers get that information? They weren't

supposed to have that. They weren't allowed in here. Where did they get it? Do you have a leak somewhere?"

"Now, calm down," Carolann advised. "Just sit down and try to relax."

But Mrs. Cohen was too worked up to stop now. "It's amazing," she said, searching frantically in her pocketbook for a cigarette. "I'm doing a fair and trying to raise funds for a school. I couldn't get publicity if I screamed. But something like this happens and now my name's all over the place."

Trying to reconcile herself to the terrible thing that had happened in her own home, Mrs. Cohen shook her head. "My little girls loved this young Japanese boy. He was like a brother. They were very close to him. You have to understand." She was not yet aware that the detectives were determined to speak to the children.

The father tried to explain: "Four years he was here. The apartment was never so safe. He brought others up here, but he would always call up and ask first. Very polite, very quiet. He would take my little girls out in the park and play with them. It's not in character... you would never think... always well-disciplined. He was into karate as a ritual. He taught it. He was a master. He was part of the family—he was..."

Mr. Cohen finally gave up trying to explain. "Ah, God, who knows, who knows, it just doesn't make sense."

Carolann was anxious to get to the little girls. In search of privacy, she steered the Cohens into a bedroom and closed the door. Minutes passed. The door opened. Carolann walked out, disgusted.

"I'll never understand people," she sighed, pressing the tips of her fingers to her temples. "Their priorities. We're dealing with someone who killed a person, someone who may have killed or injured someone else."

Mrs. Cohen returned to the dining room, sat and sipped from a cup of coffee, trying to steady her hand as she lit a cigarette. Carolann moved to her side, resuming the offensive. Like a doctor, she was probing for the right nerve, the one that would sway the woman. Carolann had two children of her own. She decided to reach out to Mrs. Cohen as another mother, a mother who must protect her children from pain.

"They're going to hear the news sooner or later, Mrs. Cohen," Carolann began softly. "Be prepared for that possibility. If they have to get bad news, it's better they get it from you. It's best that you tell them as soon as you possibly can before they hear it from other children in the street. Otherwise, they'll feel like you don't trust them. It hurts sometimes."

Mrs. Cohen nodded wearily. Carolann was beginning to penetrate. "I assure you I won't do anything to upset them. But I must talk to them." The detective sat only inches away now, her hands clasped like a penitent, her eyes at once comforting and apologetic. Her voice was barely audible.

"What would be the earliest you could bring them in to see me?"

Mrs. Cohen cradled her head in her hands, then sighed:

"Thursday."

The following day, the Japanese graduate student was taken into custody by uniformed officers after he was spotted wandering aimlessly along the West Side Highway in Harlem. Dazed and soaking wet, he had tried to drown himself in the Hudson River. It was his third attempt at suicide since the murder had been committed. The suspect was officially placed under arrest by Detective Quealy.

Several days later, Carolann and an assistant district attorney returned to the Cohens' apartment to interview their daughters. As Carolann thought might be the case, one of the little girls admitted that she had heard screams coming from the Japanese student's room in the middle of the night. But she was frightened. So she put a pillow over her head—and went back to sleep.

PART TWO

From Waitress to Detective: The Education of a Policewoman

CHAPTER SEVEN

When Carolann made up her mind to become a police-woman, two major obstacles stood in her way. First, she did not have a driver's license. And second, she lacked a high school diploma. To be eligible to take the Civil Service test for the police department, a candidate absolutely had to possess both.

So she began taking driving lessons. And, between customers at Joe and Joe's Restaurant in the Bronx, where she was still working as a waitress, Carolann would sit in an empty booth with her nose buried in textbooks, boning up on the English and history and math she needed for her high-school equivalency certificate, and beginning to familiarize herself with the basics of police procedure. A lot of cops were regulars at Joe and Joe's, and they were only too happy to give her a little on-the-spot tutoring. Especially when the pretty red-haired waitress would flash a big smile, plunk down their bottles of beer, and then inquire, ever-so-sweetly:

"Say, Jimmy, would you mind giving me a hand with this little algebra equation I was working on?"

Toward the end of 1963, Carolann filed to take the Civil Service test scheduled for early the following year. The subway ride from the Bronx down to Manhattan was an experience she would never forget. A disheveled-looking, foul-smelling man with a peculiar smirk on his face sat nearby on the train, leering at her. At her stop near City Hall, Carolann stepped off quickly, relieved to get away from him. But the man got off, too, and began trailing her. Quickening her pace, Carolann trotted up the steps of the subway station and out to the street. Her pursuer chased after and began gaining on her. Luckily, the City Department of Personnel, where the Civil Service test applications were being distributed, was only a few blocks away, and Carolann managed to dash through the front door.

The man lingered for a few moments on the sidewalk outside, muttering strangely to himself, then shuffled off disconsolately. Carolann was about to breathe a sigh of relief, but just then something very odd dawned on her. "My God," she realized, "if I ever become a police officer, I'll have to *deal* with people like that. I won't be able to run away."

Undaunted by this brush with danger, Carolann resumed her studies. In March of 1964, more than four thousand women and an even greater number of men trooped into high schools throughout the city, pencils in hand, to take the Civil Service test for the police department. Carolann sat in a classroom with forty other hopefuls, wrestling with the multiple-choice questions on vocabulary, mathematics, graphs and charts, as well as reading-comprehension drills that tested her understanding of the principles of traffic control, crime prevention, and other aspects of police work.

After two and a half hours, some of the candidates began walking toward the front of the room to turn in their completed test booklets. Carolann remained at her desk, agonizing over each and every question. When the four hours allotted for the test had expired, she looked up to find that she was the last person left in the room. Glumly, she handed in her test, convinced that she had flunked.

The next day, however, when the answers were listed in the *Chief,* a Civil Service newspaper, Carolann learned that she had scored a passing grade of 82. In those days, the police department established separate eligibility lists for policemen and policewomen. Of the 4,000 women who took the test, only 441 had passed. Of those 441, Carolann ranked 254. The police department maintained a quota of 300 women in the ranks, but there was no telling when they might reach Carolann's name. It could be months. It could be years.

She remained at Joe and Joe's, waiting for some encouraging word. It came, but not until a full year later, when the department asked her to report to her local precinct for a screening interview with one of the sergeants, who would begin the customary investigation into her character and fitness for a police job.

In the old days, the police department maintained stringent standards for new recruits. Candidates with arrest records or poor employment histories or less-than-honorable discharges from military service were automatically disqualified. Even minor indiscretions, such as truancy in school or too many speeding tickets, routinely resulted in rejections. Screening officers took a dim view of unmarried men or women who cohabited with members of the opposite sex. As one lieutenant put it, "To become a cop in New York City, you practically had to be a seminarian." Carolann was as nervous as a little girl on her first day at school when she appeared for her interview.

The interviewer was a tall, barrel-chested, jut-jawed sergeant with the map of Italy written all over his face, which seemed to be fixed in a permanent scowl. At first glance, Carolann was frightened to death. "I'm Carolann Natale," she peeped timidly.

Sergeant D'Orio, whose hulking form dwarfed the tiny desk in front of him, did not even bother to look up and answer. Instead, he just growled an acknowledgment.

Carolann brushed a crease out of her skirt, then shifted uneasily from one foot to the other, waiting for him to say something.

Sergeant D'Orio pulled out Carolann's personnel records

and slowly began to thumb through the pages, still scowling. Finally, he looked up.

"Natale," he barked, "you might as well just turn around right now, walk out that door and go back home. You don't have a prayer."

The words hit her like a jolt of electricity. Her first instinct was to cry. But then anger set in. "What do you mean, Sergeant?" Carolann demanded. "Why not?"

D'Orio held up her records in his paw-like hand, making crisp, staccato hits on the paper. He ticked off the reasons.

"Separated, but not divorced, working as a cocktail waitress, a woman living alone with two kids to support. Lady, in my opinion, you're not fit for a job with the police department. Case closed." D'Orio looked down at his desk and began to busy himself with some other paperwork.

But Carolann was not about to be written off as some irresponsible floozy. For a second, she forgot her fear and confronted the ogre head-on.

"Listen, Sergeant, I want to know what difference all that makes!" she snapped at D'Orio. "I can still do the job. I want the job because it's a good job. I think I'm competent. I want the job so I can make a better life for myself and my children."

Sergeant D'Orio looked up again, and something in his expression seemed to soften. His voice mellowed and he momentarily dropped the hard-ass act. Assuming a more businesslike approach, he began to question Carolann in detail about her family, her education, and her previous employment. It was almost as though his recital at the outset of her alleged shortcomings had been deliberately planned, some kind of cunning ploy or personality test designed to provoke an outburst and see what kind of stuff she was really made of.

After a couple of hours, Sergeant D'Orio said: "Natale, you got a long road ahead of you. Could take a year or more to do a background investigation on you. No guarantees—but I'll see what I can do."

Over the next year, Sergeant D'Orio proceeded to put Carolann under a microscope. Periodically, he would summon her back to his office for follow-up interviews, anxious to go over one detail or another in her personnel folder. In the meantime, he interviewed her friends, her relatives, her employers past and present, her teachers, her neighbors, and even her customers at Joe and Joe's. He also arranged several meetings with her ex-husband.

One of the biggest sticking points in his investigation was the matter of her two children. As a policewoman, Carolann might have to work all kinds of strange shifts and hours. Who would take care of Brenda Lee and Johnny? Sergeant D'Orio took an old-fashioned approach to cops and their families. He frowned on police parents who either neglected their children or neglected their jobs because of their children. Carolann was quick to point out that Aunt Helen had volunteered to babysit for the kids if the police job came through. But Sergeant D'Orio was not satisfied. "Let's see something in writing," he insisted. So, at Carolann's request, Aunt Helen signed a written pledge.

The screening investigation dragged on for months. Every few weeks, Sergeant D'Orio managed to find some new aspect of Carolann's life that called for an explanation, and they would go around and around on the matter until D'Orio was satisfied that Carolann had not tried to hoodwink him about some secret in her past.

One day, about a year after the probe had started, Carolann received a telephone call. "Natale," said the voice, with a familiar growl, "this is Sergeant D'Orio." Carolann immediately assumed that he had unearthed yet another unsavory detail about her that he considered potentially scandalous. But this time, the sergeant had a different purpose in calling.

"Natale, I've finished my investigation. I don't think there will be any problem now. I've approved your application and recommended you for appointment to the police force. Good luck, hope you make it."

It was a crucial victory. But there was still a long way to go. The appointment process had slowed to a trickle. The police department was hiring women no more than a handful at a time. While Carolann had now been deemed a suitable candidate, it could be years before the department's personnel division worked its way down to number 254 on the eligibility list.

In the interim, Carolann decided to take a new job. The

long hours at Joe and Joe's were taking their toll and the demands at home were becoming greater. Her babysitter's mother worked as a telephone supervisor, so Carolann arranged an interview with the phone company. A few weeks later, she swapped her apron and serving tray for the headset of a telephone operator.

At first, she handled routine requests for assistance. If you dialed "O" in the Bronx, a voice might come on the line and cheerfully respond, "Mrs. Natale. May I help you?" Then, because of her dexterity on the switchboard, Carolann was assigned to handle coin-operated calls, counseling dialers on how many nickels and dimes to drop in for their conversations. Eventually, she advanced to the prestigious position of junior supervisor, a job of such stature that it liberated her from the switchboard and allowed her to cruise up and down the aisles, headset snugly in place, ready to plug into the consoles of the other operators when there was either trouble on the line or a contentious customer who needed to be pacified.

It wasn't until 1967—three years after she had taken the Civil Service test—that Carolann heard again from the police department. This time, she was asked to report for a physical fitness test at an armory in Manhattan. From cops already on the job, Carolann knew that this test was no minor matter. Candidates might come through their character and fitness examinations with flying colors, only to be sent home because they were too flabby to do the required number of situps or too slow to run the obstacle course in the minimum time.

Carolann decided to embark on a crash exercise program. Every day, she would do sit ups and lift weights to strengthen her arms. Several times a week she would go jogging in nearby Van Cortlandt Park or do wind sprints around the wall that separated her living room from the dining room. On the day of the physical fitness exam, she was in the best shape of her life, and she passed all of the tests with ease.

There was still one last hurdle to clear before she could be appointed a policewoman—the medical checkup—and it was a cause for some concern. After joining the telephone company and working for hours at a time on a switchboard, Carolann had developed weak eye muscles. For more than a year, she had worn glasses to correct the problem. But unless she could improve her vision substantially without relying on glasses, the police department might reject her application on medical grounds.

She began visiting an eye doctor for therapy. The doctor made her stare into machines that flashed rotating lines and shapes in front of her face, movements that were designed to strengthen her eye muscles. At home, she would do exercises, holding a pen in front of her nose and moving it slowly from side to side while following it with her gaze. After a few minutes, her eyes would ache terribly from the strain. To ease the pain, she would dampen cotton pads with witch hazel and hold them over the lids.

Yet another year drifted by as she waited for the checkup, and Carolann grew increasingly discouraged.

Time was of the essence now. Despite the four long years that she had waited, she still might not make it. The original eligibility list of 441 women was starting to yellow with age and, at any moment, the city might decide to throw it out and schedule a new test for policewomen. Moreover, Carolann was now twenty-eight years old. Once she turned twenty-nine, she would be too old to take another test.

Finally, in May of 1968, Carolann received a letter asking her to report to the police department's medical section on Broadway for the final checkup. Just one hour before the examination, she was back in the office of the eye doctor for another go at the machines, hoping to strengthen her eye muscles just a little more before the crucial vision test.

A total of sixteen women were called down to the medical section for examinations that day. One flunked the test because of high blood pressure. Another was disqualified because of varicose veins. Carolann, despite her vision problems, made it through.

But then, incredibly, there was one more last-minute hitch. Of the fourteen women who had passed their medicals, only ten were to be accepted that day for training by the police department. The rest would have to return home and wait until the next batch of policewomen were appointed. It could be another six months, it could be a year. But for Carolann, fast

approaching her twenty-ninth birthday, there could be no waiting. It was now or never.

The fourteen hopefuls assembled in a waiting room. A uniformed police officer walked in with the list of finalists in his
hand. He said: "The following ten individuals have passed their
medical examinations and are ordered to report to the Police
Academy two weeks from today to be sworn in and commence
training."

The women shifted nervously in their seats. Carolann held
her breath.

The officer read off the first three names. Carolann's was
not among them.

He read off four more names. She wasn't in that batch either.
A sour, sinking sensation began to take root in the pit of her
stomach.

There were only three names left now, and the officer pro-
nounced them slowly and deliberately:

"O'Brien...

"Richardson...

"...and Natale."

CHAPTER EIGHT

The Lexington Avenue Express Number Four train rumbled south toward Manhattan, jerking spasmodically from side to side, metal scraping on metal, and screeching like a wounded animal. The train was jammed to the seams with morning commuters. Ordinarily, in keeping with the etiquette of the subway, the passengers would not have acknowledged each other's existence, avoiding all conversation and eye contact. The way to do this was to focus on the front pages of one's newspaper, bury one's nose in a steamy paperback romance, or simply shut one's eyes and snooze until arriving at the appropriate stop. But on this morning in June, 1968, most of the passengers in a certain car broke with convention by unabashedly staring at someone in their midst. So keen was their interest that one might have thought a three-headed Martian had lost its way and strayed through the turnstiles.

The object of their attention was a young woman. She was clad in a three-quarter-length, square-shouldered navy blue jacket with slash pockets and gold buttons, and a matching navy blue skirt, hem falling discreetly below the knee. She wore a white broadcloth blouse. A thin blue tie was knotted neatly at her collar and fixed in place midway down her shirt by a gold clasp bearing a miniature replica of the scales of justice. Her stockings were dark beige nylons and her shoes, black leather pumps, closed at the heel and at the toe. On her head was a broad-peaked, military-style blue cap emblazoned with a gold shield. Over her shoulder hung a regulation black leather holster bag, designed to conceal a revolver and other accessories. And pinned to the left breast of her jacket was the gold and blue shield of a New York City policewoman.

A teenager who was sitting with some friends rose and stumbled across the floor, struggling to keep his balance as the train swayed from side to side. He came within a few feet of the woman, who was clinging to a strap hanging from the ceiling. With brazen eyes, the boy slowly looked her up and down, as if she were a nude statue on display in a museum.

"You a cop?" he asked. His expression was a smart-alecky smirk.

Carolann Natale fixed the punk with a long, icy stare. "Yup."

Unnerved by this single-word affirmation, the boy seemed to lose his bravado. "You don't look like a cop," he said, and quickly retreated to his seat.

Carolann, who was heading to the Police Academy that day for a training session, knew that most of the passengers on the train probably had never seen a real live policewoman before. There were only three hundred in the entire city and, since females were still not permitted to go out on patrols, most of the policewomen were in low-visibility jobs, doing matron duty or working undercover assignments. But Carolann was neither embarrassed nor annoyed by the stares. In fact, she was quite pleased with the way she looked in her new uniform. The last time she had worn a uniform, she was a rosy-cheeked little girl, going to classes with the nuns at St. Lawrence O'Toole grade school in Brewster.

Training for Carolann and her nine classmates was for the

most part perfunctory. As a rule, police recruits were required to spend four to six months at the academy, boning up on community relations and human behavior, techniques of patrol and traffic direction, criminal procedure, and the use of firearms. But in the late 1960s, the department was anxious to rush new recruits into the field as quickly as possible. The idea was to let them get their feet wet with a little on-the-job training, then bring them back a few months later for additional classroom instruction. Consequently, Carolann spent only two weeks at the academy before she was shipped out to her very first precinct, the Forty-second in the Bronx. Or, in the police vernacular, the "four-two."

Her first day in the new precinct began on a macabre note.

After the cops on the 8 a.m. to 4 p.m. shift had turned out for roll call, one of the sergeants buttonholed Carolann. "Welcome to the four-two, Natale," he said with a smile. "You got here just in time. Not fifteen minutes before you walked through that door we got a report of a female DOA up on the Grand Concourse. Old lady who lived by herself. Guess who gets to go up there and do the search."

"Oh no," said Carolann with a grimace.

"Must be your lucky day, Natale," chirped the sergeant, who was enjoying watching this rookie policewoman squirm.

"DOA," as Carolann had learned at the academy, meant dead on arrival: police jargon for a corpse. It was standard procedure for the cops to search all dead bodies, removing cash, wallets, rings, necklaces, earrings, watches, and other valuables, and vouchering them until they could be claimed by the next of kin.

However, the police department was extremely skittish about who searched whom. While male officers would search male DOAs, only females were supposed to search female DOAs. Carolann had known that sooner or later she would have to conduct such a search. But for somebody who had always cringed at going to wakes to view the deceased, it was going to be queasy business, nonetheless.

A senior policewoman accompanied Carolann and another rookie to the scene to show them the ropes. As the older woman preceded the two recruits up the stairs, Carolann saw the woman's knees begin to shake. "Good God!" she thought to herself. "If that's what it's like after twenty years on the job, what's it gonna be like for me in my first year on the job?"

Luckily, the first DOA search went off without a hitch. The body was clammy and cold, the color of chalk, but there was no trace of blood or decay and Carolann managed to control her revulsion. In fact, the sergeant back at the precinct was so pleased with how she comported herself at the scene that he rewarded her by sending her out on another DOA search on her second day at work. Once again, she handled the assignment with poise.

On her third day in the four-two, the sergeant greeted Carolann, grinning as usual. "Guess what, Natale."

"Don't tell me," she sighed, refusing to believe her beginner's luck. "You got another report of a female DOA and I gotta do the search, right?"

"Catch on fast, dontcha?" The sergeant was practically beside himself with glee.

The first two searches had been relatively simple. The victims had died of natural causes and were discovered soon after by friends or relatives. But Carolann was not prepared for what awaited her on the third search. It was a sight so jarring, so revolting, that she nearly quit the force altogether.

On that awful day, Carolann drove to another apartment in the Bronx. An old lady had been living there alone with her dog, but nobody had seen a trace of either for about a month. A fetid odor had begun to drift from her apartment, growing more pungent each day, and the neighbors finally summoned the police to investigate.

By the time Carolann arrived, the male cops already had battered down the door. Carolann stepped inside the darkened apartment, pinching her nostrils to fend off the stench. One of the male cops was standing near the entrance, filling a bucket with ammonia-soaked rags to kill the odor. At first, Carolann could see little. But then, as her eyes adjusted to the dim light, she spotted it. Across the room, in all its gore, a corpse was sitting upright in a chair, its flesh blackened by decay. The head and torso and limbs had been swollen into grotesque, balloon-like shapes by the body gases released during decomposition. Like an overcooked egg, the belly had exploded, spilling blood and rotting innards over the floor, now crawling with maggots.

And that poor starving dog, desperate for life-sustaining nourishment, just sat there, eating its master's entrails.

The nightmares just wouldn't go away.

Every time Carolann tried to sleep, the grisly scene replayed itself in her mind—the corpse, the maggots, the dog. Some nights, she would bolt upright in her bed, trembling and soaked in a cold sweat. It wasn't worth it to be a policewoman, she began to tell herself, not if she had to face that kind of thing again. She would rather quit the job and go back to waitressing. For days, Carolann agonized over what to do.

Ralph, her cousin's policeman-husband, had a suggestion. Ralph worked in the Emergency Service Squad, the department's dirty-work-and-daredevil unit. Emergency Service cops clambered up the cables of bridges when psychos threatened to leap, fished bloated corpses out of the rivers, and scraped suicide victims off the subway tracks, so Ralph had seen plenty of mangled bodies.

"Look, Carolann," he said. "You can't refuse to do a DOA search. You can't turn down an assignment. But you can ask for an oxygen mask before you go into a building to do that search. Next time you go to the scene and you get a whiff of odor, tell the sergeant you want a mask.

"Now, just between you and me, the only people who carry oxygen masks are Emergency Service cops. So they're gonna have to call for an Emergency Service truck to get you that mask. If they call for the truck, mention my name to some of the Emergency Service guys. They know me. They may even tell you to stay outside, they'll do the search for you. Worse comes to worse and you gotta do it yourself, at least you got that mask to wear so you won't get sick."

Ralph's suggestion was a godsend. In Carolann's mind, it gave her a crutch, an "out," a way of reasserting some control over a situation that seemed to have spun completely beyond her control. Armed with the knowledge that she could call for an oxygen mask if she had to—and delay conducting the search until the mask arrived—Carolann found she had the strength of mind to go on. Over the next four years, there would be more assignments to search female corpses. Oddly enough, not once would Carolann find it necessary to demand an oxygen mask.

Searching dead bodies was unquestionably the most unpleasant assignment given to rookie policewomen. But searching live ones was no picnic, either.

Whenever females were taken into custody and brought back to the four-two for booking, it was the policewomen who were obligated to pat them down for weapons or drugs, sometimes concealed in delicate places. One morning, about 2 a.m., two male cops brought in a scruffy-looking hooker. As they hustled her up to the front desk, she began to scream and curse and kick out at the two officers, indignant over the rude treatment she felt she had received.

Carolann was guarding the female detention pens that night. "Got one for you, Carol," said one of the cops.

By allowing the prostitute to have some candy and cigarettes in her cell, Carolann managed to calm her down. The woman was grateful for this small kindness and reciprocated by letting Carolann do the mandatory search, picking through her tangled hair, inspecting her soiled clothing, prodding her pockmarked skin.

An hour later, the phone near the female detention cells rang. It was the sergeant on the front desk. "Carolann, those two officers who locked up that pross are on their way back to the precinct to pick you up. Lieutenant wants all three-a-yas to take a run over to Lincoln Hospital and get shots for infectious hepatitis and syphilis. That doll you searched? They think she's a carrier."

And that morning, just as the sun was rising over the Bronx, one extremely cross policewoman limped slowly back into the stationhouse, nursing a painfully throbbing backside.

In many ways, being a rookie was like pledging a fraternity. Every day, it seemed, you had to endure some new and perverse form of hazing. One of the most annoying assignments was bleacher duty at Yankee Stadium, which was situated not far from the precinct. Every week or so, Carolann and a handful of other officers would be dispatched to the seats in center field, where the underprivileged children were seated for home games. It was the cops' responsibility to keep peace among the young ruffians, who were inclined to indulge in fist fights, shoving matches, and other acts of rowdiness on the average of once an inning. A favorite pastime was pelting the outfielders on the opposing team with debris or attempting to dump soda on their heads as they leaped to rob a batter of a home run. Cruising up and down the aisles, Carolann would scan the crowd with an eagle eye, trying to ignore the catcalls and whistles and other crude gestures that were offered expressly for her benefit.

One day, after Carolann had turned to watch Mickey Mantle step to the plate, an empty beer can came whizzing out of the crowd and bounced off the top of her head. With murder in her heart, she whirled around, determined to catch the culprit, but all she found was a sea of smirking, giggling faces, any one of which might have committed the dastardly act. An arrest was impossible. It was like looking for a needle in a haystack.

The thing that troubled Carolann most about her first few years as a policewoman was that she seemed to have so little time to spend with her children. Her schedule was erratic; she often had to work nights and sleep days. Even if she could manage a few hours with the kids, invariably she would have to turn them over to the babysitter at the end of the day, then rush to the precinct to report for duty. It was an arrangement that always left her feeling guilty.

Sometimes, when she came home from work, the babysitter would excitedly report: "Oh, Carol, you'll never guess what little Johnny said last night! It was just so cute! If only you had been here to hear it."

Reliving her children's most precious experiences through the recollections of their babysitter was hardly the ideal approach to motherhood. Carolann felt she was shortchanging the kids, and shortchanging herself as well.

During the summers, however, the police department gave an assignment to the policemother that made life a bit more bearable. When Carolann was detailed to Orchard Beach, a public recreation area on the shore of Long Island Sound, she took Brenda Lee and Johnny along for the day. While her own children built sand castles at the water's edge, Carolann was on duty, keeping an eye out for lost toddlers. When the strays were found wandering around on the beach, they would be brought to a fenced-off area with a carousel-like roof, where Carolann would try to keep them calm and occupied until their parents arrived to retrieve them. It sounded like a dream assignment—except that many of the little angels turned out to be unruly brats who would respond to her tenderness by kicking, biting, screaming, wetting their pants, or throwing up on her. On July Fourth, when some two hundred lost children ended up in the kiddie compound, Carolann was ready to pull her hair out.

One Sunday in the summer of 1970, Carolann had about fifteen tiny wards in her custody when somebody heaved a bottle over the fence. It crashed just a few feet away from one of the children. Carolann looked up just in time to see a brick come hurtling through the air from another direction. Hurriedly, she ushered the children back under the protective canopy. Suddenly, a shower of bricks and bottles began to rain down upon the compound, as if the entire area were under siege. From her vantage point, Carolann could see dozens of cops on scooters, converging on the beach. Fists were flying, and people were shouting and running in a dozen different directions.

When one of the scooter cops rode by, Carolann signaled frantically for help.

A few minutes later, an enormous police panel truck backed up to the compound, and Carolann began escorting the little ones out from under the canopy. Braving the barrage of rocks and bottles, she ran them out, two and three at a time, and put them in the back of the truck. When all fifteen had been evacuated, Carolann herself jumped on. After the truck pulled away from the combat zone and moved to a more secure location on the fringes, Carolann learned from other officers that she and the children had been in the center of a full-scale riot, touched off when a policeman tried to arrest a man for possession of drugs on the beach.

Later that night, as the violence subsided, grateful parents came by to pick up their children and thank the young policewoman who had shepherded them to safety.

CHAPTER NINE

Picture Times Square on a crisp fall night in 1971.

Red and gold neon signs, flashing and flickering and undulating from all sides. Billboards, larger than life, touting everything from Camels and Cokes to fried chicken and "Girls! Girls! Girls!" Broadway theaters and movie houses, porno shops and peep shows, cut-rate clothing stores and camera marts, penny arcades and pizzerias, malodorous souvlaki stands, greasy lunch counters, and the sleaziest of sleazy saloons.

Now, picture the cast of characters.

Well-heeled theatergoers, rushing to make the curtain. Gawking tourists, overwhelmed by it all. Uniformed cops, mounted like cavalrymen on enormous horses or standing at street corners twirling their wooden batons and casting a suspicious eye on all who pass. Hustlers, con artists, shills and skells. Fuzzy-headed drunks leaning precariously against walls.

Cripples and old men sprawled on the sidewalks with grimy palms extended. Incense burners and pretzel vendors and fast-talking peddlers, ready to sell you everything from Third World newspapers to cheap plastic flowers to iridescent necklaces and hula hoops to toy whales that paddle around in a tub of water and squirt geysers through the tops of their heads. Shoeshine boys and long-haired street musicians. Transistor radio freaks and young dudes idling under the marquees, mumbling and jive-talking and slapping each others' palms in soulful greetings.

Over on Eighth Avenue, the ladies of the evening are out in numbers. Sashaying up and down the street, their hips swaying seductively, they scan the passing crowds for prospective customers. Sometimes, they stop and linger in the doorways of curio shops or Greek restaurants, striking an alluring pose and hoping to snare a big spender for a quick tumble.

"Goin' out tonight, sweetie pie?" asks a bosomy black woman in her sultriest voice. She is wearing spiked high heels and an outrageous blonde wig and she flutters a pair of eyelashes that look like giant spiders.

A middle-aged man carrying a briefcase takes the bait and steps up to negotiate the price. A moment later, the black woman is clutching him demurely by the elbow, and they stroll around the corner to the five-dollar-a-night fleabag hotel to transact business.

A few doors down, another young woman is standing in a darkened doorway, studying the passersby with cool detachment. She is clad in a tight, form-fitting blouse, miniskirt, and white leather boots. Despite a thick frosting of rouge and lipstick, her face is quite attractive.

An older couple walks by, heading toward one of the legitimate theaters on the side street. The man turns to leer at the woman in the doorway. His fur-coated wife gives him one of those under-the-eyebrows scowls, then yanks him sharply by the arm. Picking up the pace, she drags her red-faced husband down the street like a forlorn puppy.

A moment later, a younger man passes by the same doorway. He spots the woman and decides to make an overture.

"Hi," he says.

The woman is wary. She looks first to the left, then to the right before giving a tentative reply. "Hello."

The man grows bolder. "Whatcha doin' here?"

She cannot lie. "Workin'."

The man smiles slyly. "How much?"

But it is a coy game this woman plays. "For what?" she asks.

The man steps closer and lowers his voice to a murmur. In hushed tones and graphic detail, he spells out exactly which pleasurable acts he would like her to perform.

"How much can you spend?" wonders the woman, knowing that the first rule of the business is to let the buyer bid low, then raise the ante.

"Twenty-five dollars," answers the man.

For an instant, the woman glances just past his shoulder, to a spot a few doors up the street. Then she gives a telltale nod.

The man smiles again, his anticipation building. "Can we go now?" he asks. He is unaware of the three burly men who have stepped out from another doorway and are quietly moving up behind him.

"Mister," says the woman, with a new and surprising tone of authority to her voice, "I'm sorry to tell you that the only place you're goin' tonight is the stationhouse. You're under arrest." From her shoulder bag, she whips out something blue and gold and shiny.

It's a policewoman's badge.

"Whaa?" mutters the man, startled and confused. And then the realization sets in: he has just propositioned a cop. Terrified, he staggers backwards. Right into the arms of the three plainclothesmen who have anticipated just such a reflex response.

"Tough luck, pal," says Carolann Natale, the decoy prostitute who has just collared her first unsuspecting john of the evening.

Working the "pross detail" was one of those assignments that policewomen loathed. The city was in the midst of a campaign to crack down on vice and clean up Times Square, a never-ending crusade that seemed to gain fresh impetus every time a new mayor took office. In addition to rounding up the streetwalkers, the police department had decided to sabotage their trade by busting their patrons. So, on a rotating basis, policewomen were ordered to disguise themselves as prostitutes and arrest at least two johns a night. The female officers felt demeaned and degraded by these assignments. One woman was so resentful that she showed up for duty in her regulation navy blue uniform, knowing perfectly well that in that guise she could hardly pass for a streetwalker. An angry captain promptly lodged an official complaint against her and ordered her to go home. Meanwhile, a story was circulating that a policewoman in Detroit who had refused to work the "pross detail" had been suspended on the spot for dereliction of duty.

Periodically, Carolann was borrowed from the four-two precinct in the Bronx to do decoy work in Manhattan. She hated the assignment as much as any of the other women but, like the DOA searches, there was no way to refuse it. Instead, she decided to make her arrests as quickly as possible on each tour, then come straight back to the stationhouse to busy herself with paperwork for the rest of the evening.

There was no question that the worst part of working the "pross detail" was standing on some corner and posing. Not that there was any danger: a back-up team of two or three male cops was always a few feet away, camouflaged among the loiterers and winos. But all those indignant stares and clucking tongues from the women who were convinced that Carolann was out there peddling her body were humiliating. Sometimes she would have to stifle the urge to blow her cover and just shout out: "Hey, lady, don't look at me like that. I'm not a prostitute, I'm a cop. I'm just as good as you are."

While deceiving the passersby was all too easy, deceiving the competitors—the real prostitutes—was not. Seasoned hookers seemed to have a sixth sense about cops and could make the decoys as soon as they set foot on the street. Sometimes, they would berate Carolann: "What you comin' back here for, woman? You done made your collar already. Now you interferin' with our business!" Scattering like a flock of frightened pigeons, the hookers would regroup on another corner, just up the block.

One Christmas Eve, Carolann and her back-up team arrested a young law student after he propositioned her on the street. The next day, as they were coming out of court after the arraignment, the law student turned to her and said: "I don't care if you are a cop. Would you have dinner with me anyway?"

While the offer was flattering, Carolann declined. As she joked to the other cops: "Suppose I did have dinner with that guy and we ended up liking one another. Just think, maybe we would have gotten married and had children. And they would have had children. And one day one of my grandchildren would have come up to me and asked, 'Grandma, how did you and Grandpa meet?'"

Most of Carolann's "clientele" were businessmen and professionals. One of the men who propositioned her was the owner of a well-known fast-food chain in New York City. Another was a construction company executive. A third was a researcher for a company that manufactured typewriters.

The going rate for a "date" was twenty dollars, although one lovesick suitor generously offered Carolann one hundred and fifty dollars if she would spend the whole night with him.

One night, as Carolann was lurking in her favorite doorway along Eighth Avenue and Forty-eighth Street, a car cruised by. As it neared Carolann, the driver slowed for a long, lingering look. Then he accelerated and turned the corner. A few minutes later, the same car returned for a second pass. Again the driver eyed Carolann with keen interest. Again he drove around the corner.

A moment later, after parking the car, the man behind the wheel came sauntering around the corner on foot and headed straight for Carolann. After all that window-shopping, it looked like he was finally ready to talk turkey.

"How much, honey?" he asked.

In order for Carolann to have legal grounds to make an arrest for soliciting for purposes of prostitution without committing entrapment, the john would have to mention a price as well as an explicit sex act. Discreetly, she maneuvered to draw him out.

"Well," she answered, "how much are you willing to spend?"

The man smiled wanly. "Two ninety-eight."

"What!" snapped Carolann, insulted by such a meager offer.

The man tried to make amends. "Listen, honey, it's not that I'm cheap or anything like that. It's just that I hadda spend five bucks to park the car and I'm gonna have to spend another fifteen for a hotel room. So all I got left is two ninety-eight."

"Listen, mister," said Carolann, her ego still smarting, "just what do you think you're gonna get for your two ninety-eight?"

The man proceeded to reel off a lengthy list of sex acts, omitting nothing from the repertoire.

That did it. A bargain hunter.

"Mister," said Carolann, "I got some news for you. This is what you get for two ninety-eight!"

With that, she pulled out her police badge and placed the poor fellow under arrest.

In February, 1973, Carolann was transferred out of the four-two in the Bronx to Midtown South, a rough-and-tumble precinct in the heart of Manhattan.

As a policewoman, it was Carolann's job to do matron duty, searching and guarding the female prisoners who were lodged overnight at the precinct until they could be arraigned in criminal court the following morning. Most of the prisoners were streetwalkers, rounded up en masse by the undercover men of the public morals squad or by the uniformed patrolmen, and on busy nights the policewomen might have their hands full with fifty or sixty ladies of the evening. The girls were a bawdy and boisterous lot, strutting, jabbering, and cursing, clamoring for coffee or candy or cigarettes the moment the policewomen locked them into their cells.

Veteran cops were inured to their ways and even learned to talk their language. Sometimes, officer and prisoner would lapse into shop talk, discussing mutual acquaintances.

"Hey, Tootsie," began a detective as he was fingerprinting a hooker one night. "I hear Little Alice got the clap."

"The clap?" Tootsie began to chortle. "Honey, she not only got the clap, she got the applause and the standing ovation, too!"

And both the detective and the prostitute burst into laughter.

Do-gooders, reformers, and amateur social workers were in

for rude treatment by the prostitutes. One night, Carolann made the mistake of trying to shame a young black hooker into seeing the error of her ways. "How can you do this?" she asked the girl. "How can you sell your body?"

The prostitute gave Carolann a pitying look, then shook her head. "Shit, woman, you dumb. *Dumb!* At least I gets money for it. But you jes' gives it away for nothin'!"

And that was the end of that.

The most difficult part of being a matron was doing the search. Prostitutes often concealed marijuana joints, penknives, or razor blades in their purses, clothing, or even the orifices of their bodies. As soon as a policewoman ventured near, they would begin to squawk like chickens.

"Oh, don't be doin' that," a girl might protest as Carolann reached for her purse. "The policewoman the other night didn't go lookin' in there. Nobody else makes me do that. Now you ain't got no cause to be lookin' in my purse, officer. Don't you be touchin' that. . . ."

Patiently, Carolann would persist. "Now, c'mon, honey, you know I gotta look in there. You're no stranger around here; you've been locked up plenty of times before. You know the rules."

The basic rule of thumb in doing a search was that you could never judge a book by its cover. Appearances could be deceiving. It was not uncommon for a police matron to suddenly discover that the female she was searching was not really a female after all. Transvestites and transsexuals, many of them more attractive than the prostitutes who were biologically female, often fooled the arresting officers and drifted into the female cells.

After a tour of duty, Carolann and her friend Hester Bellomo, who was also a matron, would retreat to a coffee shop and swap war stories.

"God, Hester," Carolann began one morning, "last night I had a real beaut. A case of the hand is quicker than the eye. They bring in this girl for me to search. So I make her take the blouse off, then the bra, and I could see it was a female. So now, the bottom part; I tell her to drop the pants. She turns around and takes her hand and pushes what she's got in the front to the back. But her hand was so fast, I swear to God, that when she turned around I didn't even see it.

"Then the arresting officer comes back up and he says to me, 'I think we made a mistake.'

"'What kind of mistake?' I ask.

"'I think we got a male in the female cells,' he says.

"'Oh, no, no way, impossible,' I say. 'I personally search all my girls.'

"So we go back to the cells and, sure enough, he recognizes her. 'You!' he shouts. 'What the hell you think you're doin' in there? You're supposed to be in the male cells!'

"But the girl says, 'Oh, no, I'm stayin' here. The policewoman says I can stay here.'

"I take another look at her and I ask, 'Hey, are you a female . . . or a male?'

"'Well!' she says, all huffy-like. 'You searched me, didn't you?' I tell you, Hester, this girl was so quick with how she moved her clothing and her, er, equipment, I just never thought. These guy-gals or gal-guys or he-shes or whatever you want to call them, they have it down pat. They don't want to go in those male cells, no way."

Hester began to chuckle. "I had a couple similar to that. One time, the officer says to me, 'You know, I'm not really sure whether it's a female or not.' So I said, 'Don't worry, I'll find out.' The prisoner went in the cell and I stood by the door. You don't know how many contortions I had this one going through. It was unbelievable. I don't remember how the heck he did it, but I finally wound up having him lay down on the bench and put his feet up in the air. It was so unbelievable how this guy was hiding everything. But finally, I was able to spot it."

Hester was really rolling now. "Best one, though, was the time they brought this one in and he's prancing around outside the cell. 'All right,' I say, 'remove your blouse, remove your bra.' Well, he removed his bra with such pride! He just stood there and"—Hester made a cupping gesture with her palms, like she was juggling two grapefruits—"Arrumph! Just stuck right out there from all those silicone injections."

Carolann laughed so hard she nearly spilled her coffee. Hester continued merrily.

"He says to me, 'You see? I *told* you I'm a female.'

"I said, 'That doesn't prove anything to me. Drop your pants.'

"So then he starts pouting. 'Well,' he says, 'all right, if you wanna be that way, I'll just go in the male cells.'

"Can you imagine?" said Hester. "Thought he was going to impress me with all that silicone. Some nerve that one had."

Some of the impersonators and borderline cases would kick and scream and bawl like babies in an effort to remain in the female cells. But, in time, Carolann perfected a method for quickly and quietly ending disputes and coaxing them into the male cells.

"Anybody who claims to be a female and wants to remain in the female cells can stay as long as they produce a doctor's certificate proving that, legally, they are now women," Carolann would declare.

A simple little requirement. Nobody could really take issue with it.

The only thing that Carolann neglected to mention was that no such certificate existed.

CHAPTER TEN

One humid night in August of 1974, an attractive, young artist named Rita Smith returned home to her Greenwich Village apartment after a dinner date with her boyfriend. Flushed and weary from the heat of the evening, she was looking forward to lingering under the shower, then turning in early for bed. It was fifteen minutes past midnight when Rita walked through the door.

The apartment was a spacious two-bedroom, occupying the entire basement floor of a red-brick townhouse. The church next door owned the townhouse, and for many of the tenants that arrangement seemed to guarantee an extra measure of security.

After flipping on the lights, Rita locked the front door and walked into her bedroom. She had started to unbutton her blouse when she heard a familiar meowing, coming from the other bedroom.

"Samantha! Come here, Samantha!"

Stubbornly, the cat ignored her calls.

Walking to the far end of the hall, Rita found that her pet had planted itself near a closet and was hunched on all fours, sniffing purposefully at the base of the door. The door appeared to be snugly shut.

"Silly cat," Rita scolded, running her hand along its furry black back. "You must be hungry. Looking for food, aren't you?"

A flicker of a shadow passed along the floor, just under the closet door, but only the cat seemed to notice.

"Come with me, kitty," murmured Rita as she scooped the creature up by the scruff of the neck and began stroking it behind the ears. Walking back into the kitchen, Rita opened a can of tunafish, and the cat soon became engrossed in eating its dinner.

Once the cat had been fed, Rita finished undressing and headed for the bathroom.

With the bathroom door opened halfway to let the heat escape, Rita turned on the shower faucets, moving them back and forth until she had regulated the temperature of the water. Then, casting aside her robe, she stepped inside the tub and drew the plastic curtain closed. Rita shut her eyes and luxuriated in the delicious warmth of the water, allowing her muscles to relax and her thoughts to drift drowsily, oblivious to the world outside.

Suddenly, an unseen hand tore back the shower curtain. Rita whirled. Then she screamed.

A man stood there, watching her. He had no face. Only a horrible nylon mask, stretched tight over his head, grotesquely distorting his features. In his hand he held a long knife with a curved blade.

It was a nightmarish replay of that grisly moment in the movie *Psycho*, when Janet Leigh is stabbed to death in her shower. Only this time, it was really happening. He was there, in front of her, holding that knife, staring.

"Don't scream," hissed the voice behind the mask. "If you

make another sound, I'll kill you." Covering her naked body with her arms, Rita cowered in a corner and started to tremble.

"Wash the soap out of your hair," ordered the masked intruder. His speech was accented. "Now dry yourself."

The masked man's eyes were riveted to her body. He was clearly becoming aroused. With a sweep of his knife, he motioned her out of the bathroom, down the hall toward the front bedroom.

"Lie down on the bed," he commanded. "Turn your face toward the wall."

The man removed his dungarees and his short-sleeved shirt. Then he peeled off his mask and crawled onto the bed with Rita. He began biting her on the neck.

"No, don't," she sobbed, but she was too terrified to resist.

He started babbling, whispering that he had seen her before, in her blue dress, riding the subway, carrying her books and papers. "You got a good shape," he mumbled, growing more and more excited. His body reeked of sweat and grime. "Get me hot," he moaned.

And then he raped her.

Between grunts of passion, the rapist turned inquisitive. "How old are you?" he asked.

"Twenty-three."

For some reason, her answer startled him.

Abruptly, he stopped what he was doing, jumped off the bed and began to put his clothes back on. He pulled his mask back over his face and reached for his knife.

"Walk back to the bathroom," the rapist ordered. Numbly, Rita obliged.

He followed her through the bathroom door. Inside, the tiles were still wet from her shower and the mirror over the medicine chest was clouded from the steam. The rapist began to study Rita's body, not with lust this time but with the meticulous eye of a physician examining a patient.

"Wash off," he told her. "Wash good. Let's not leave any evidence for the police. Besides, I don't want you to get gonorrhea."

Rita stepped back into the shower and turned on the faucets. She began to soap her body.

But the rapist was not satisfied. "More!" he shouted at her. "More! More! More!"

Finally, he relented. "That's enough. Stop. Now stay here for twenty minutes." Drawing his knife close to her throat, he warned: "If you move before that, I'll come back and kill you."

And then he was gone.

From somewhere outside, a door slammed.

Twenty minutes later, when Rita ventured out of the bathroom with a towel wrapped around her, the apartment was empty. Still trembling, fighting back the tears, she made her way to the front door and locked it. The first person she telephoned was her boyfriend. He promised to rush right over. And then, at long last, she allowed herself the one consolation possible after her ordeal.

She began to weep.

After spending five years searching dead bodies, masquerading as a twenty-dollar-a-tumble streetwalker, and playing nursemaid to female prisoners, Carolann had welcomed the transfer to the Manhattan Sex Crimes Unit. For some time, she had been convinced that she had more to offer the police department. Now she was finally getting the chance to prove it.

Working in sex crimes gave her the opportunity to conduct her own investigations. And, since the unit fell under the aegis of the Detective Bureau, the assignment might eventually lead to a detective's badge and a raise.

One of the first things she had to learn, however, was that rape reports were occasionally suspect. Sometimes, the women who brought charges turned out to be prostitutes who were cheated by their customers. Sometimes, the complainants were jilted lovers, desperate for revenge. And too many times, a case was unprosecutable under the law because the police were unable to prove that force was involved.

But there was no question that the attack on Rita Smith was a clear case of rape.

Carolann and her partner, Detective Bob Magnusson, knew that the girl had a legitimate complaint as soon as they began interviewing her. She broke down several times while rehashing the details of her attack. Her boyfriend was the first person she called after the attack, a perfectly normal reaction; victims always seek out people they can trust. And that horrible moment in the shower, when the knife-wielding masked man yanked back the curtain. Over and over again, Rita told the investigators: "I thought I was dead." And all too clearly, Carolann could imagine the terror that Rita felt.

Despite her anguish, Rita managed to provide Carolann and Magnusson with a fairly detailed portrait of the rapist. About five-foot-ten, slim, wearing a striped, short-sleeved knit shirt and dungarees. After he removed his mask, she had seen a man fifteen to twenty-five years old with a small, round head, short brown hair, a mustache, and dull, droopy eyes. His accent was Hispanic and he looked and smelled dirty.

With the police at her side, Rita walked from room to room in her apartment, slowly reenacting the crime. A few days later, she visited police headquarters, where a female detective in the Sex Crimes Analysis Unit constructed a composite likeness of her assailant. Using an Identikit, a device in which clear plastic strips displaying a wide variety of facial features can be assembled to match particular descriptions, the detective, at Rita's direction, selected the contour of the face, then added the jaw, the eyes, the nose, the mouth, the ears, and the hair.

Armed with the composite, Carolann and Magnusson began canvassing the neighborhood around Rita's apartment. None of the neighbors or passersby recognized the face. Neither did the custodian at the church which owned Rita's building. But the custodian did make an interesting comment: A couple of maintenance men who worked for the church might have had access to a spare set of keys to the girl's apartment. Carolann decided to interview the superintendent of the church buildings to get more details.

The next day, Carolann visited the super to ask about the two maintenance men. The super described them, but neither was tall enough to match the description given by Rita. Then, as an afterthought, the super added:

"Oh, there was another fellow around here who did some work for us. I think he was the nephew of one of my regular men. He wasn't here for very long, though, only about a month or so."

"What did he look like?" asked Carolann.

"Tall, thin. Had a mustache."

"Do you remember his name?"

The super thumbed through some records on his desk. "Yes, here it is. James Melendez. They used to call him Jimmy. He only lives a few blocks away from here, over on Tenth."

Five minutes later, Carolann was inside the lobby of a ten-story apartment house on Tenth Street, scrutinizing the names on each of the mailboxes. There was a Melendez on one but, oddly, it did not seem to correspond with any of the apartment numbers under the buzzer. She decided to step outside to have a look around.

On a stoop at the rear of the building, a little girl was sitting and playing with her doll. She was dressed in shorts and sneakers and her long dark hair was braided into neat pigtails.

Carolann smiled at her. "Hello, honey. Do you know a Mr. Melendez?"

The little girl looked up at the pretty lady and flashed a big grin, baring a brand-new gap in her front teeth. "Yes, that's my daddy. He's the super here."

"Which apartment do you live in, honey?"

"Right here!" beamed the little girl. "This is our house. That's my mommy in the kitchen." And the little girl dashed up to the screen door to announce the visitor.

Inside the kitchen, a woman dried her hands on a dish towel and walked toward the door. She looked to be at least eight months pregnant.

"Yes?" the woman said.

Quickly, Carolann concocted a cover story. "Oh, I'm looking for a friend of mine who used to live in this building." Deliberately, she chose a name that she knew was not on the mailboxes. "Marianne Gomez."

The woman looked perplexed. "I don't remember her, but maybe my husband does. I'll get him. Jimmy! Jimmy, come here!"

Jimmy shuffled out from the bedroom in his slippers, weaving unsteadily from side to side and trying to keep the rum in his tumbler from sloshing over the sides of the glass and onto the floor. Tall, thin, short brown hair, mustache, droopy eyes. The moment Carolann saw him, she knew she was standing face to face with the *Psycho* rapist.

Again, Carolann asked for her fictitious friend, Marianne Gomez.

"No, nobody here by that name," answered Jimmy, swaying like a hula dancer.

"Gee, that's strange," said Carolann. "Well, I'll just have to try to get some more information about her. Is it okay if I come back later?"

Jimmy gave her a leering grin. "Sure, any time. Anything I can do to help."

Carolann walked calmly around to the front of the building, toward a waiting car. Another policewoman had been sitting behind the wheel, and she looked up with a questioning expression.

Unable to contain herself any longer, Carolann smacked her right fist into her left palm and blurted out right then and there:

"I found him!"

The problem with trying to arrest Jimmy on the spot was that Carolann did not have sufficient evidence. Jimmy bore a remarkable likeness to the composite put together at police headquarters. But composites are merely tools to assist investigators; they are never admissible as evidence in court.

The best way to seal the case against Jimmy would be to have Rita pick him out of a lineup. There was only one small hitch. Since Jimmy had not yet been charged with any crime, he was under no obligation to stand in a lineup. The police could request him to do it—they could even beg him—but they couldn't force him. And if he refused, there was not a thing they could do about it.

The investigators in the Sex Crimes Unit decided to try a ruse to coax Jimmy into a lineup voluntarily.

Two days later, Carolann returned to Jimmy's apartment with Detective Magnusson. Jimmy and his wife welcomed her back like a long-lost relative. But they were dumbstruck when Carolann and her male companion flashed police badges in front of their noses.

"Listen, Jimmy," Carolann began. "A young woman was raped inside one of the buildings that belongs to the church. We know that you once worked there, and we know you had access to the keys. But we don't think you're the guy who did

it. Besides, the victim probably can't identify the rapist anyway. Still, we'd like to eliminate you once and for all as a
suspect. Would you mind coming back to the stationhouse to
stand in a lineup? It will help us find the guy who really was
responsible."

It was a gamble, but it worked.

"I gotta go with the police," Jimmy told his wife. "I'll be
back in a little while."

Back at the offices of the Sex Crimes Unit, the other investigators scurried about to find stand-ins for the lineup. Most
of the stand-ins were police officers in civilian clothes. But
there was also a pair of down-and-out derelicts, lured by the
promise of a five-dollar bill. All told, there were seven in the
line-up, including Jimmy. Each man was asked to hold a large
piece of cardboard in front of his chest. Each piece of cardboard
bore a different number.

Standing in the room next door behind a one-way mirror,
Rita Smith studied the men.

"Look at each person carefully," Carolann told Rita. "If you
see the man that assaulted you, tell me the number he's holding
up."

Rita's eyes moved down the line, from the first man, to the
second man, to the next man, and right past Jimmy without a
flicker of recognition.

Crestfallen, Carolann decided to try another tack.

"Rita, I'm going to have each subject come up close to the
window, turn sideways, and then walk back to his place. Look
carefully again, and then tell me if anyone looks like the rapist."

When the parade ended, Rita turned to Carolann. "I think
it's number three." Carolann fought to conceal her excitement.
Number three was Jimmy. But then Rita added: "Or it could
be number five."

Now, Carolann was gripped by a growing sense of defeat.
With Rita seesawing back and forth on an identification, she
knew that her case against Jimmy was about to fall apart.

"I'm sorry," said Rita. "I just can't tell. Maybe if I could
hear him . . . talk . . ."

One of the other investigators had an idea. Perhaps they
could establish a case through voice identification. The door

to the lineup room was opened, just a few inches, and Rita was asked to stand outside and listen. Then, to assure fair treatment for the suspect, the order of the men in the old lineup was scrambled and each of the subjects was given a different number. Finally, each subject was told to utter the same phrase within earshot of the girl outside. The words, painfully familiar to Rita, were:

"Wash off. Wash good. Let's not leave any evidence for the police."

Rita whispered to Carolann: "It sounds like number six." Once again, she was leaning toward Jimmy. But then, as before, she started to hedge. "But I just can't be sure."

Carolann was disgusted. Leaving Rita behind for a moment, she muttered to one of the other detectives: "Damn it! He did it! I know he did it. We can't let him beat this rap."

They decided to try one last tactic before letting Jimmy wriggle off the hook. After the other stand-ins in the lineup were sent home, the investigators took turns talking to Jimmy. First, Detective Magnusson. Then Detective Dan Haley. Then Carolann. Finally, all three at once.

Carolann resorted to a deliberate lie. "Listen, Jimmy, that girl has positively identified you as the rapist." But then she took a disarmingly conciliatory tone. "But she doesn't want to see you go to jail. She doesn't want us to lock you up. What she really wants is for you to apologize. That was a terrible thing you did to her. Whaddya say, Jimmy? Why don't you do the decent thing and apologize to her?"

"I didn't mean it," Jimmy whimpered. "I didn't mean to rape her. I'm a burglar, not a rapist."

Tears in his eyes, Jimmy began to give the investigators a full confession, telling them that he had broken into Rita's apartment through a rear door. He had only intended to steal a television set and some dolls, but Rita came home unexpectedly early and surprised him. In a panic, he had dashed into the closet in the bedroom. He could hear the cat sniffing at the door. Then footsteps approaching. A woman's voice. In a sadly comic admission, Jimmy told the police, "I was so scared in that closet that I wet my pants."

When the woman entered the bathroom and turned on the

shower, Jimmy decided to make his getaway and started out of the closet on tiptoes. But once outside, something caught his eye.

Steam, billowing out from the bathroom door.

It was dangerous, he knew, but he just had to take a quick peek.

And there she was, behind the shower curtain, the young woman he had lusted for ever since he saw her on the street. He could see the contours of her naked body. He couldn't stop himself. He yanked the curtain back.

"Please don't kill me," she had begged, and her pleading had aroused him even more. "I'll do anything . . ."

When it was over, Jimmy agreed to sign a full statement, admitting to the rape. Then, looking up at the investigators, he sniffled, "Now can I do it?"

Carolann cocked an eyebrow.

"Do what, Jimmy?" she asked.

Jimmy wiped his nose on his sleeve.

"Now can I apologize to the girl for what I did?"

CHAPTER ELEVEN

During her first two years in the sex crimes squad, Carolann often found herself working cases alone. Most of the men in the squad simply did not want to be burdened with women partners. The prevailing sentiment was that women were physically weak, emotionally flighty, and totally undependable in those life-or-death situations that every cop dreads. The department might have given them shields and revolvers, but in the eyes of the men, the women were far better off behind a typewriter or a filing cabinet than they were behind the wheel of a squad car or the stock of a shotgun.

Many of the detectives in the sex crimes squad were younger men who were anxious to move on to more prestigious units, such as homicide. In those days, sex crimes was considered a low-priority assignment by the Detective Bureau. With blunt disdain, some of the bosses dismissed it as "a left-handed outfit."

The detectives in the squad knew that the best way to get out was to make a good showing by boosting their clearance rates, that is—the percentage of cases deemed solved. And the best way to do that, they were convinced, was to team up with a rough, tough hotshot who could back you up and bail you out, not some silly broad who might fret about mussing up her makeup and getting a run in her stockings while chasing a two-hundred-pound sex maniac down a dark alley.

So, shunned by the men, Carolann became accustomed to working solo.

One day, a new face appeared in the office. He was a barrel-chested detective in his early forties with the craggy good looks of a professional quarterback and a pair of powerful, ham-sized hands. His manner was boisterous and boastful, and from the very outset he made it clear that he took a dim view of authority in general—and squad commanders in particular.

The scuttlebutt on Charley Valois was that he was coming to the squad "under a cloud." He had developed a reputation as a troublemaker, ever since he was bounced out of a homicide squad because of a little scrape with the lieutenant in charge.

For many of the detectives, a transfer from homicide to sex crimes was like being sent from the New York Yankees down to a farm club in West Cupcake, Montana, and the other investigators in the squad viewed the new arrival warily.

But to Charley Valois, sex crimes was just another assignment from a department that neither understood nor tolerated his particular brand of individuality, something he had grown used to over the past twenty years. Charley had worked everything from vice to drugs to a precinct to homicide. Unlike the younger detectives who were striving to get ahead, Charley already had spent two decades in the trenches and was winding down his career. He really didn't care what squad they assigned him to, as long as he still managed to get a piece of the action. Twenty years after he had first put on a badge, Charley still had a rookie's zest for police work. He loved being a cop almost as much as he loved life itself.

On his first day in the sex crimes squad, Charley cheerfully trotted into the office and extended his massive right hand to each of the detectives who was working that tour. Glancing into a side room, he noticed a sexy-looking woman, wearing black boots and a tight green dress, sitting at a desk.

"Who's that?" whispered Charley. "A victim? Looks like a hooker."

"Guess again," laughed one of the detectives. "That's Carolann Natale. She's a policewoman with the squad."

And, on that less-than-encouraging note, Charley Valois first met Carolann Natale, the woman who would become his partner for the next two years. It was hardly a match made in heaven.

In the entire police department, two more different personalities did not exist. They were like Officer Day and Officer Night. Carolann was an ambitious young policewoman on the way up, determined to do well and earn her gold detective shield. With her superiors, she demonstrated the utmost respect. Her reports were perfectly typed, usually in triplicate. And she followed proper police procedure to a tee. Charley, on the other hand, was a crusty, street-smart veteran who preferred to break down doors first and ask questions later. He made no attempt to disguise his contempt for the bosses, whom he regarded as glorified paper shufflers. He generally neglected to type up any reports at all. And proper police procedure in his book was whatever procedure he happened to have been using for the past twenty years.

Carolann had heard about Charley's reputation as a troublemaker and, at first, she was leery of him. But nobody else in the squad was anxious to work with her and she needed a partner. So she decided to chance it and ask Charley if he would like to help her on a case. Charley had never worked with a woman before and he had no idea of how to deal with one at this stage. But he had tried everything else in his career and she looked like she could use all the help she could get, so, what the hell, why not give it a shot?

The first time they teamed up together was almost the last time. It nearly turned into a disaster.

A ten-year-old girl had been raped by her stepuncle, and Charley and Carolann drove up one night to his apartment in Spanish Harlem to make the arrest. His wife admitted them to the apartment; the suspect was asleep. The two investigators tiptoed down the hall, toward the bedroom.

Charley nudged the sleeping man by the arm. "You better get up, pal, we're the police. You're gonna have to come back to the stationhouse with us."

The man shook himself awake, then sat up in bed. "I ain't goin' nowhere," he said. "You ain't got no warrant, you can go fuck yourself. My home is my castle."

It was just about then that Charley noticed the dagger lying next to the man, on the sheet. Whether it was the dagger or whether it was the stepuncle's smartass response or whether it was the heinous crime he had committed, something inside Charley snapped. It all happened so fast—Carolann had no time to react when Charley slammed the bedroom door shut, right in her face.

Inside, it sounded like World War Three had started. Fists smacked into flesh. Bodies bounced off the walls, grunted and groaned, then thudded to the floor. Furniture scraped and skidded across the room.

"Open this door!" screamed Carolann, furious that Charley had locked her out and, at the same time, fearful that he might be in serious danger. Drawing her revolver, Carolann screamed again: "Damn it, Charley, open this door right now! Lemme in!"

Suddenly, the ruckus inside came to an abrupt halt. The lock snapped back and the door slowly opened. Out sauntered Charley, looking a bit rumpled but otherwise unhurt. His prisoner, however, had not fared so well. The poor man was bloodied and bruised and his hands were cuffed securely behind him.

Carolann was seething. "Don't you ever do that to me again!" she raged. "I'm your partner, Charley. I have a gun. I can help. For God's sake, don't just think of me as a female. What would you think if I slammed the door in your face? Suppose I needed help? Wouldn't you be angry?"

Charley was taken aback by the outburst. He began to hem and haw. "Oh, gee, all right—I'm sorry." But he had to admit it: She was absolutely right.

It was the first, but certainly not the last clash the two investigators would have over the best way to handle cases.

For example, as they were soon to learn, Carolann and

Charley had radically different approaches when it came to questioning rape victims. Carolann would conduct precise, painstaking interviews, carefully laying a proper foundation for each succeeding question. But Charley would sometimes disrupt her train of thought by jumping in with a question that was totally out of left field. With the victims, Carolann was somber and serious, treating their ordeals with delicacy and discretion. Yet, Charley would tease the girls and tell them jokes, trying to break the ice and befriend them.

"You shouldn't do that, Charley," Carolann would scold.

"Yeah, yeah, you're right, Carol." After a while, Charley decided that the best way to deal with Carolann was to "yes" her, then do exactly what he had wanted to do in the first place.

Sometimes, Charley would make up lists of things that needed to be done on a particular investigation. Carolann would immediately tear the lists up, then nudge Charley to attend to matters that she considered more pressing, only to provoke Charley into complaining: "Stop pushin' me, will ya?"

Even in restaurants, they managed to argue. Charley, always the gentleman, simply could not endure the sight of a female dinner companion handing money to a waiter, even if that female happend to be his partner. Whenever he and Carolann took a meal break together, he would quickly reach for the bill before Carolann had a chance to take out her wallet.

After several weeks of free dinners, Carolann realized that Charley, who had seven children of his own to support, would soon go broke if he continued with this foolish chivalry. "Listen, Charley," she finally said. "This is ridiculous. You and I are gonna be working together a long time. That's a lot of meals and a lot of money. You have to let me pay my share."

Finally, they agreed to a compromise. Charley would continue to pay all the bills. But once they were outside the restaurant and back in the car, Carolann would settle up with him, fair and square.

Charley had a devilish sense of humor, and he delighted in making his new partner the butt of his jokes. Every time they entered a precinct where the uniformed cops were about to book some prostitutes, Charley would grab Carolann by the arm and start bellowing: "All right, honey, move it along, let's get in there, don't give me a hard time!"

"Stop that!" Carolann would shout, mortified by the looks she was getting from the other officers in the stationhouse.

And Charley, a sly grin on his face, would roll his eyes up into his head and cluck his tongue: "Got another one here for you, boys."

Once, Charley, Carolann, and another female police officer went to interview a rape victim in a cheap West Side hotel that was notorious as a haven for five-dollar-a-trick hookers. Just as the three investigators left the building, a taxi driver cruised by and stared at the trio with intense curiosity, obviously aware of the hotel's seedy reputation.

Charley just couldn't resist.

Placing both arms around the shoulders of the two police-women, he began strutting down the steps and affected the lascivious smirk of a man who has just enjoyed a tryst, *menage à trois*. With eyes wide as saucers, the cabby jumped the curb and nearly crashed into the side of the hotel.

As the only male detective willing to work with Carolann on a full-time basis, Charley often had to suffer the jibes of the other men in the squad. During a meal break one night, as Charley, Carolann, and two other detectives were walking along Third Avenue toward a parked squad car, one of the detectives began to get on Charley's case.

"C'mon, Valois," he needled. "We know who does all the heavy lifting in this team. You do the driving. You get the gas. You take care of the car. Carolann just sits and watches, right?"

But Charley quickly came to Carolann's defense. "Hey, that ain't true. She's completely liberated. She does everything." And then, in a dangerous boast, he added: "She even changes the tires."

Sure enough, when the four investigators reached the car, the left rear tire was as flat as a pancake. The two other de-tectives turned expectantly toward Carolann, folded their arms, and broke into big grins. But Carolann was glaring angrily at Charley. In fact, if looks could kill, at that moment she would have been guilty of murder. For the truth was that she had never changed a flat tire in her life.

Charley, however, was not about to be proven a liar. "C'mon, Carol," he whispered, "you can do it. Let's show these bums. I know you can do it. Just follow my instructions; it's a cinch. Now, get the jack out of the trunk and take off the hubcap . . ."

As Carolann went down on her knees and started to tackle the flat, one of the men detectives guffawed: "My wife should be here to see this!" Carolann began to mutter under her breath.

Just as Carolann got the car jacked up and the flat removed, a drunk stumbled out of a tavern. Bobbing and weaving like a prizefighter, he staggered woozily down Third Avenue, taking one step backward for every two steps forward. The detectives watched with fascination as he zigzagged toward them, occasionally circling the sidewalk in figure-eight patterns.

As he neared the squad car, the drunk struggled to focus his gaze on all the activity. When he spotted Carolann down on the ground, his expression turned to astonishment. He studied her closely, blinking his eyes a couple of times in case it was a hallucination. Mouth agape, he turned to look at the three men who were standing nearby and watching. Then, he turned back to Carolann.

"Jeshush Christ!" the drunk exhaled. "A woman changing a flat tire! Wash thish world comin' to?" And shaking his head like a man who has just crossed paths with a herd of pink elephants, the drunk zigzagged back up the street, heading toward the tavern.

"That'll sober him up," chirped Charley.

"You and your big mouth," fumed Carolann, whose hands were now coated with black grease.

Even routine errands had a way of turning into unanticipated adventures when Charley the Prankster was around. When Carolann was called down to the Internal Revenue Service for an audit, she made the mistake of taking Charley along for the ride. At the IRS office, a woman auditor began to question some expenses on which Carolann had taken a business deduction. Just as Carolann opened her mouth to explain, Charley beat her to the punch by playfully cautioning the auditor:

"Don't believe a word Carol says. She's lying through her teeth."

"Charley!" gasped Carolann, totally aghast.

The auditor was not amused. Charley simply grinned.

Out in the field, their cases occasionally became slapstick escapades reminiscent of the Keystone Cops. One day, Carolann spotted a rape suspect standing with a friend on the corner of 125th Street in Harlem.

"There he is!" she shouted. Like a whippet, Charley raced after them. Carolann was two steps behind. Just then, her heel got caught in a crack in the sidewalk and down she went, flat on her face.

The rapist veered off into a liquor store while his friend continued straight ahead. Unaware of Carolann's plight, Charley caught up to the friend, locked him firmly in a half-nelson and marched him back to the squad car. He was stunned to find his partner sprawled on the pavement, her clothes disheveled, her hose ripped, and her knees bloodied.

"What happened to you?" asked Charley. "Stop to take a nap?"

Carolann rose painfully and started to brush the dirt off. "Some partner you are!" she snapped. "You leave me flat on my face on 125th Street, and you come back with the wrong guy. He's not the rapist. The rapist ran into the liquor store."

Charley's face turned beet red. He quickly released the friend, and the two investigators headed back toward the liquor store, where they placed the real culprit under arrest.

Ordinarily, Carolann and Charley would work all phases of an investigation together, one backing up the other. But one night, Charley decided to go off with some uniformed cops to track down a pimp in Times Square, and he left Carolann behind at the hospital to interview a rape victim. It was the first time that the two partners had split up on a case since they had started working together. Carolann was miffed at Charley's haste to desert her.

An hour later, Charley came wobbling back into the emergency room at the hospital, dazed and moaning. Two uniformed officers were holding him firmly under the arms to keep him from falling.

"What happened to you?" asked Carolann.

"You won't believe it," sighed Charley, holding a hand to his head. "I got hit with a bowling ball."

"You got hit with *what?*"

"We go into this hotel, looking for that pimp. I walk into his room and—Whammo!—the guy's got a bowling ball sitting on top of the door, rigged up like a booby trap."

Luckily, the X-rays of Charley's skull showed no fractures. But Carolann, who was usually the victim of Charley's ribbing, could not resist turning the tables. "See what happens?" she chided, as the nurse was bandaging Charley's head. "First time you go out on a case without me, and you get beaned by a bowling ball."

Although Carolann and Charley disagreed vehemently and often about the best way to proceed on their investigations, they soon discovered that, in an odd way, their different styles complemented one another. They began to trust each other's instincts, even if it meant following up a hunch that looked like a long shot. As Charley would tell Carolann: "If you got a feeling that a guy's gonna show up on the Brooklyn Bridge with a parachute at three o'clock in the morning, then I'll be there with you at three o'clock—lookin' for him to fall."

While Carolann couldn't match Charley's muscle, she had other, more subtle skills that Charley learned to appreciate. For one thing, she was adept at interviewing rape victims, especially children. And she had a knack for defusing potentially violent situations with feminine charm. Never was Charley more grateful to have Carolann along as a partner than the time they drove up to Central Park West to question a suspect about the rape of a young Harlem girl. Just as they were about to enter his building, a squad car from the local precinct cruised by. One of the uniformed cops recognized Charley.

"Need any help?" he asked.

"Nah, we can handle it," replied Charley, with his customary humility. The squad car drove off.

Charley stepped up to the suspect's door and rapped firmly. The door opened, and standing behind it was a six-foot-seven-inch, three-hundred-pound weightlifter with biceps so massive they looked like they were about to split the seams of his T-shirt.

"Yeah?" snarled the giant, glaring down angrily at Charley.

"Oh, Jesus," Charley thought to himself. "What the hell do

we do if this is the guy who committed the rape?"

Without a moment's hesitation, Carolann stepped between the two men. Looking up demurely at Goliath, she flashed a big smile. "Excuse me, sir," she began in her most ladylike voice, "I wonder if we could just ask you a few questions?"

The big man looked down at the pretty policewoman and softened. From hulking ogre, he turned into docile pussycat, and he politely answered each and every one of Carolann's questions. Moreover, Carolann concluded that he was not the man who had committed the rape.

Charley breathed a deep sigh of relief.

During the two years they worked together, Carolann and Charley cracked hundreds of cases. They arrested a television network executive who lured two little boys up to his apartment with the promise of new bicycles, then forced both youngsters to commit sodomy. They arrested a French fashion photographer who forced himself on a young model during a session at his studio. They arrested a man who raped his blind woman neighbor. They arrested a con artist who picked up an airline stewardess at a singles bar and then drugged her with sodium pentothol so he could take advantage of her. They arrested a child molester who prowled the city's parks in search of little boys. And they arrested five of the twenty-five teenagers who gang-raped a prostitute at an Oriental social club.

But of all the crimes that Carolann and Charley investigated, none generated greater outrage among the public—and the police—than the sad case of the young girl who was walking her puppy, one cold night just before Christmas, 1976.

CHAPTER TWELVE

It began routinely.

According to the initial report, filled out with customary dispassion by the uniformed police officers who first responded to the crime scene, "Complainant Jenny Miller, female, white, twenty-two, out walking her dog, was forced to the roof, raped, and robbed by three perps."

The attack reportedly had occurred in Manhattan's Ninth Precinct, a dismal ghetto on the Lower East Side where the tenements are aged and crumbling, the vacant lots are strewn with empty beer cans, rusting bed springs and the fetid carcasses of dead cats, and the sentinels of poverty loiter for hours on street corners, glassy-eyed and listless, slurping noisily from green pint bottles concealed in small brown paper bags.

The rape complaint was automatically referred by the Ninth Precinct to the investigators in the Manhattan Sex Crimes Squad, but at first glance the case seemed suspect. Why would a young woman be out walking her dog late at night in one of the worst sections of the city? With characteristic cynicism, the sex crimes investigators guessed that the complaint might be bogus, or perhaps the work of a disgruntled hooker who decided to call the police when her client refused to pay up.

Carolann and Charley were just finishing up a four-to-midnight tour when the case came in. Despite the lateness of the hour and their doubts about the veracity of the complaint, they decided to drive to Bellevue Hospital, where the uniformed officers had taken the complainant for a medical examination. If she had, in fact, been raped, it was essential to interview her as soon as possible to obtain the most vivid details of the attack, and hopefully, the most promising leads.

It wasn't something perverse that led Carolann and Charley to press the victims of sex crimes for such lurid information. The acts and language used by a rapist, no matter how vulgar, constitute a modus operandi, or method of operation. Since most sex criminals are repeat offenders, they often duplicate the same pattern of behavior and speech in each attack. That pattern may tip the police to their identities and lead to an arrest in cases that have gone unsolved.

Inside the emergency room at Bellevue Hospital, the two investigators found a young white girl with long brown hair, clad in a white surgical gown and curled in a fetal position on an examining table while a doctor nearby prepared a syringe with an antibiotic injection. From moment to moment, the girl whimpered and shivered, drawing her fingers into tight fists close to her mouth. Ugly welts and bite marks covered her neck. Her eyes were clouded in a vacant stare.

"Suffering from exposure," one of the nurses quietly explained to Carolann.

There was little doubt now that the girl had been raped. Charley stood back a few steps as Carolann made the first overture. "Jenny," she began, pulling her police badge from her purse, "I realize that you've been through a terrible ordeal, but we have to ask you a few questions."

The girl's gaze drifted towards Carolann, but her eyes held a faraway look. "I don't know why they had to do that to my dog," she mumbled, almost hypnotically. "I don't know why . . ."

Carolann was puzzled. "What happened to your dog, Jenny?"

For a moment, Jenny stared blankly. Then, as if something inside had fractured, all the features of her face seemed to collapse and she burst into tears. "They killed him!"

Jenny was starting to become hysterical. Abruptly, Carolann backed off. At almost the same time, the doctor rushed to Jenny's side, this time with a sedative in hand.

Unable to continue the interview, Carolann and Charley decided to return to the crime scene to search for evidence. The two uniformed officers who had accompanied Jenny to the hospital were still waiting outside the emergency room, and they agreed to come along and assist with the search.

The rape had occurred on the roof of a grundgy six-story tenement in the heart of the Ninth Precinct. There was no elevator in the building, so the search party was compelled to use the staircase. At the fourth floor, Carolann stopped to rest her legs and catch her breath.

"Why is it that every case we get is on the top floor?" she wondered aloud.

But Charley could only smile wanly, too winded to reply.

At the top landing, the investigators pushed open a heavy metal door and stepped outside into the icy night air. Patches of snow covered the tarpaper roof. The temperature had plummeted into the teens and a bone-chilling wind whipped savagely around their legs. Turning up the collars of their overcoats, the four cops flicked on their flashlights and fanned out across the roof.

"Over here!" shouted Charley. The others came closer.

Behind a chimney, he had found a torn blue T-shirt and some bobby pins. Nearby, one of the uniformed cops spotted a hair clip and a pencil holder. And tied to one of the exterior vent pipes was a green dog leash. The loose end of the leash had been slashed in half.

If the dog had been killed, there had to be a body. It wasn't in the street; the cops could see that by peering over the edge of the roof. At the rear of the building they found an airshaft. Maybe it was in there. One of the uniformed officers walked back through the metal door and descended the stairs to the ground floor.

At the bottom, he found a brick wall with a hole in it. By wriggling through the hole, the officer was able to make his way into the airshaft. From the rooftop above, Carolann, Charley and the other uniformed cop could see the beam of his flashlight, bouncing eerily on the ground.

Suddenly, a shout echoed up the shaft.

"I found the dog! The dog is dead!"

By the next day, Jenny had recovered sufficiently for the investigators to make another attempt at an interview. During a visit to her apartment, Carolann and Charley found her to be articulate, intelligent, and an unlikely resident of the rundown neighborhood. Jenny worked as a salesgirl at a local pet shop, but her real ambition was to become a veterinarian. More than anything else in the world, she adored animals. In fact, she had been out walking her cocker spaniel puppy when she was attacked.

"Can you tell us what happened?" Carolann asked softly. And as Carolann and Charley sat listening, Jenny slowly re-created the terrible events of the night before.

She had returned to her building about 7:30 p.m. after walking the puppy. A teenage boy was loitering outside near the steps, but she paid him little heed and reached for her key. Suddenly, he was at her heels, bounding up the steps. Quickly, Jenny inserted her key in the inner door. But just as quickly, the youth was at her side with a knife in his hand.

"Don't make any funny moves," he warned. "Now, give me all your money."

Jenny reached into her pocket and found fifty cents.

"Shit, is that all you got?"

The boy began to search her, allowing his hand to roam freely over her body, fondling her breasts.

"All right, bitch," he hissed, "inside." The mugger turned the key that Jenny had left in the lock, pushed open the door and shoved the terrified girl and her dog into the hallway.

In the vestibule he grabbed her from behind and placed one hand over her mouth. With his other hand, he pressed the knife up against her throat.

"Now, we gonna walk up to the roof," he murmured, forcing the girl and the dog toward the stairs.

It was bitter cold on the roof, but the youth was too worked up to stop now. After tying the cocker spaniel to a vent pipe, he pushed Jenny behind a brick chimney and unbuttoned her coat. Then he inserted the knife into the neck of her T-shirt and, in a single motion, tore it open from top to bottom.

"Take off your clothes, bitch," he commanded. At the same time, he dropped his pants to his shoes.

Twice he raped her. Once he sodomized her. During the attack, he teasingly drew his knife down the side of Jenny's cheek, across her chest and belly, cutting off bits of her pubic hair, threatening to sexually mutilate her.

"How does this feel?" he asked, his face wreathed in a sadistic grin. "Sharp, isn't it?"

The door to the roof clanged open, and two younger boys appeared. The rapist glanced up and recognized familiar faces. He shouted to the two boys in Spanish. It looked like the whole thing had been prearranged.

Leaving Jenny naked and shivering behind the chimney, the rapist pulled up his trousers and walked over to join his friends. The two younger boys leered at Jenny, snickering and joking with the older boy, whom they called Chico. With an audience now, Chico walked back toward Jenny and raped her a third time. Then, one of the younger boys took his turn.

Standing off to the side, Chico began to pace back and forth, like an animal that smells danger in the wind. When he noticed that the roof door had inadvertently slammed shut, he began muttering and cursing, blaming the two younger boys for this lapse. His eye fell upon the puppy, still tethered to the vent and whining in the cold.

Suddenly, like a madman, Chico bounded across the roof, slashed the green leash with his knife, and yanked the poor creature up by the neck.

"I'm going to get rid of this fucking dog!" he hissed, just loud enough for Jenny to hear. Struggling and choking, the dog pawed the air furiously as its head began to slip through the collar.

Jenny's eyes widened in horror. "No!" she pleaded. "Please, please don't kill my dog! Oh, please!"

But her pleading seemed to excite Chico even more, turning him on, driving him to torment the woman he already had violated. Eyes gleaming, a demonic smile on his lips, he dangled the puppy over the air shaft.

"Nooooo!" screamed Jenny, totally beside herself. And at that instant, Chico let out an insane laugh and hurled the puppy to its death.

In a frenzy now, crazed with his own blood lust, Chico shouted at Jenny: "Get up! Get over here by the edge! I'm gonna make you jump down where I threw the dog. Jump, bitch, or I'll cut you to pieces!"

He started toward her with his knife. Suddenly, the youngest boy stepped in front and blocked his path.

"Don't be fuckin' crazy, Chico," the boy cautioned. "You talkin' about murder. That's twenty-five to life, man."

Chico hesitated for a moment, pondering his friend's words. Then he seemed to regain his senses.

"Bitch!" he snarled, backing off to another side of the roof.

The youngest boy had saved Jenny's life, but he did not intend to go unrewarded for his act of valor, so he raped her, too. She was beyond caring now, mind and body deadened to all further abuse. In a modest gesture of compassion, the boy allowed Jenny to warm herself with her overcoat after he had finished with her. He even put his arm around her shoulders to shield her from the cold.

"Remember," he whispered in her ear, "you owe me a favor. I saved your life."

Chico strutted back across the roof with Jenny's blue jeans in his hand. "What are these for?" he asked, jangling a set of keys that he had found in one of the pockets.

"The pet store where I work," she whimpered, drawing the overcoat tighter around her shivering body.

Chico was intrigued. "Do they have Dobermans there?"

Jenny nodded.

"Then get dressed, bitch," said Chico. "You're gonna take us over there so I can get one." A few minutes later, the trio of young rapists marched Jenny down the fire escape and up the street.

At the pet shop, the two younger boys waited outside while Chico forced Jenny through the front door. After he made Jenny open the cash register, he greedily scooped out all the coins and bills. Then, strolling the length of the shop, he ran his grimy fingers along the outside of the cages, teasing the frightened animals that were locked inside. About three-quarters of the way down he stopped in front of one particular cage. Inside, was a black and brown Doberman pinscher puppy.

"Open it," Chico commanded. Jenny obliged. Chico dragged the dog out by its paws, dropped it on the floor and began to play with it roughly.

Walking toward the rear of the store, Chico spotted still more booty—a calculator and a stereo set. Ignoring Jenny and the dog for a moment, he began to dismantle the speakers.

It was when he turned his back that Jenny bolted for the door.

Chico heard the footsteps and whirled. Pulling his knife from his belt, he raced after her. "Bitch!" he screamed.

But Jenny was too quick for him. She yanked the front door open, stepped outside, and—just as Chico came within grasp—slammed the door shut. Chico clawed savagely at the handle, only to discover that an automatic mechanism had been tripped when the door closed. He was locked in, and there was no way out.

Once outside, Jenny began shrieking wildly. When the two younger boys realized that she had broken free, they turned on their heels and fled.

The restaurant next door was still open, and Jenny collapsed into the doorway, weeping hysterically. One of the waiters quickly telephoned the police. Within seconds, the sirens of the approaching squad cars began to wail.

Suddenly, from the pet shop next door, came an ear-shattering crash. The waiters in the restaurant ran to the windows.

Trapped by the locking door and panicked by the approaching sirens, Chico had made a desperate leap through the plate-glass front window. Shards of glass were everywhere, glittering on the sidewalk and on the pavement.

And running up the street went the young rapist, the Doberman puppy squirming and yelping under his arm.

* * *

The gang rape of Jenny Miller at knifepoint was one of the most odious cases investigated by the sex crimes squad, all the more appalling because of the savage slaying of the victim's puppy. The newspapers gave special attention to that senseless act of cruelty and, oddly enough, even Jenny herself seemed more distressed by what had happened to the dog than what had happened to her.

With Jenny's help, police artists prepared a sketch of Chico that portrayed an Hispanic youngster with a medium afro, a pockmarked complexion, and fierce, feline eyes. A partial sketch was done of one of the younger rapists, but the only telltale feature was the pair of dark-framed eyeglasses he had worn. Jenny was unable to supply enough information for the artists to render a likeness of the third young rapist.

Carolann and Charley concluded that the two younger rapists probably lived in the neighborhood. One of the neighbors had told Jenny that she had seen three boys milling about on a street corner just before the attack, and she had recognized two of them as being from nearby streets.

After the sketches were completed, Carolann drove Jenny back home from the squad office. It was late in the afternoon, around the time that school let out. On an impulse, Carolann decided to cruise the neighborhood, hoping that one or the other of the younger boys might be on his way home—and that Jenny might spot him.

And suddenly, as they turned a corner, there he was. The kid with the glasses, walking nonchalantly into a tenement on East Fifth Street. "That's him!" blurted Jenny.

Alone with the victim and without another officer to back her up, Carolann decided not to risk an arrest. Instead, she jotted down the address of the building on a slip of paper and tucked the slip in her handbag.

The next day, Carolann and Charley drove to the local junior high school, where they interviewed the principal and several teachers. Without divulging details of the rape, they described the two younger boys and asked if any of the teachers could recall male students who had been unusually disruptive or unresponsive in class lately.

"You know," said one of the ninth grade instructors, "there

is one kid who comes to mind. I can't seem to get through to him in class. He's distant, remote. Always seems withdrawn. I think he hates me. The other reason I remember him is that something very strange happened just the other day."

The teacher began to chuckle. Carolann and Charley waited patiently for him to continue.

"Of all things," explained the teacher, "this kid asked me if I would like to have a Doberman pinscher puppy for Christmas."

Carolann immediately asked for the boy's name and address.

The teacher glanced at some files. "George Jimenez, 634 East Fifth Street."

Unobtrusively, Carolann reached into her handbag and pulled out the slip of paper, the one bearing the address of the building which the young boy with glasses had entered a day earlier, just as Jenny pegged him as one of the rapists.

The slip said: "634 East Fifth Street."

George Jimenez was still in his pajamas when his grandmother admitted Carolann and Charley into their modest apartment on the morning after Christmas. In the corner of the living room, a small Christmas tree twinkled. When the two investigators told George he was under arrest for rape, he seemed contrite, yet relieved. George was fourteen years old.

With George in tow, Carolann and Charley walked several doors up the block to the apartment of a neighbor, Mrs. Carmen Corales. Just as Mrs. Corales opened her door, the stolen Doberman puppy ran into the living room, panting heavily and leaping wildly at the human visitors. After stealing the dog, Chico had sold it to Mrs. Corales for fifty dollars.

"Sorry, lady," said Charley, scooping the pooch up in his arms and heading for the stairs. "This dog is stolen property and we have to take him." Charley cuddled the pup and it lapped at his face with its wet, pink tongue.

Back at the offices of the sex crimes squad, the other investigators broke into gales of laughter when Carolann and Charley walked in with the purloined pup.

"Evidence in a rape case," said Carolann, keeping a perfectly straight face.

"What's he gonna do?" wondered one of the detectives. "Testify?"

As one of the investigators poured some milk into a saucer, another scurried off in search of food. Meanwhile, the puppy raced gleefully around the office, yipping and yapping, darting under desks and nipping at feet. Then, in all the excitement, he urinated on the floor.

Based on information obtained from George, Carolann and Charley tracked the second younger boy, Jose Lopez, to the apartment of an aunt who lived in Chinatown. Later that night, they arrested Jose without incident. Jose was thirteen.

Since both George and Jose were under the age of sixteen, the police were legally obligated to summon their parents or guardians before reading the youngsters their rights. By nightfall, a throng of relatives had crowded into the youth squad room in the Thirteenth Precinct, where the investigators were pressing the two younger boys to give up the real name and address of the third and most savage of the rapists—Chico.

Of the three rapists, Jose had been the least brutal, the one who had talked Chico out of killing Jenny and the one who had sheltered Jenny from the cold. Carolann and Charley stressed that a judge would certainly take these actions into account as mitigating factors when it came time for sentencing. And, after much weeping and shouting among the assembled relatives, two of George's uncles finally prevailed upon Jose to cooperate.

Carolann handed the police sketch of Chico to Jose. "That's him," nodded the boy. "Except he's bald now. He shaved off all his hair. He's been staying in Connecticut with some relatives, but he'll be back in town tonight."

And that night, just as he was walking up the steps to his apartment, Chico was taken into custody by detectives from the Ninth Precinct.

Because of their ages, both George and Jose were prosecuted in family court and sentenced to eighteen months each in juvenile detention facilities, the maximum permissible under state law.

However, sixteen-year-old Benito Rivera—alias Chico—was vulnerable to much stiffer punishment as an adult. In March of the following year, Rivera appeared in state supreme court.

At first, he admitted to robbing Jenny, but he procrastinated on confessing to the rape.

"In that case," announced the female assistant district attorney, "we're ready to go to trial right now."

Five minutes later, after consultation with his lawyer, Rivera admitted to the rape, too. Asked by the judge why he had thrown the puppy from the roof, Rivera said simply: "I hate dogs."

On the day of sentencing, the defense attorney asked that Rivera be given "youthful offender" treatment, a designation that could have resulted in a relatively lenient sentence of four years or less. The lawyer portrayed the youngster as a deprived child who had grown up in a tough neighborhood and was so disturbed that, at one point, he had even considered hanging himself. With proper counseling, the lawyer maintained, the boy might be rehabilitated to lead a productive life.

The judge listened patiently to the lawyer's arguments—and promptly rejected the request.

"The people of this community must be protected from predators like you," he sternly told the defendant. "You obviously had many disadvantages in life, but you knew the difference between right and wrong. You must be held to account for it."

With that, the judge sentenced Chico to twelve years in prison.

Over a period of eighteen months, Carolann and Charley worked together on more than two hundred sex-crimes cases and solved the vast majority. Their clearance rate (percentage of cases deemed solved) soared to eighty percent—among the highest for any pair of partners in the Manhattan Sex Crimes Squad. Their personnel files grew thick with letters of commendation from superior officers, and letters of gratitude from victims whose cases had been solved. Some of the other investigators in the squad made crude jokes and lewd innuendoes about the real purpose of the partnership, but Carolann and Charley simply shrugged them off. Let them talk; the only thing that counted were results. Although they might have started their partnership as the Odd Couple, Carolann and Charley had clearly proven that they were an effective investigative team.

Despite her successes as an investigator, however, there was one thing that eluded Carolann: a gold detective shield. Charley already was a detective. But as late as 1977, after she had spent four years in the Detective Bureau, Carolann still held the rank of police officer. There had been promises of a promotion and a raise that would have amounted to $2,300 over three years. But those promises went down the drain in the spring of 1975, when New York City was rocked by a major fiscal crisis. Faced with the prospect of bankruptcy, City Hall slashed spending drastically and forced severe economies upon all city agencies. In the police department, entire units were disbanded and five thousand younger officers were laid off from their jobs. Meanwhile, veteran cops who were anxious to move up found their careers suddenly stymied by a mandatory freeze on promotions. For Carolann, a gold shield began to look like a distant dream, more out of reach than ever.

The crisis did not begin to ease until the spring of 1977, when the department started to rehire batches of laid-off cops. Promotions were resumed, although they seemed to trickle down from headquarters at a snail-like pace. With rekindled hope, Carolann waited each day for that telephone call or communique from "downtown" that might bring word of her promotion.

Early one morning in June, 1977, as she was preparing to leave home for work, the phone in the kitchen rang.

"Carol?"

It was one of the detectives in the sex crimes squad. Her anticipation began to build. Could this be it? "Oh, hi, what's up?" replied Carolann, struggling to maintain a tone of nonchalance as she waited for the good news.

But on this morning, the detective had news of another sort, something totally unexpected. "It's Charley. He's in the hospital. He had a heart attack."

Stunned beyond words, Carolann listened numbly as the detective on the phone gave her the details. It had happened late the day before, just after Carolann and Charley had finished a particularly grueling tour of duty. Driving home alone after work, Charley had felt a sharp pain stabbing through his chest and he began gasping for each breath. Luckily, he had managed to drive himself to the nearest hospital. But the diagnosis was grim: a massive coronary.

At first, he was kept in isolation. Days later, when he was moved out of intensive care and into his own room, Carolann was permitted to see him. In preparation for the visit, she stuffed a shopping bag with books and magazines, a miniature backgammon set, and a couple of pints of Charley's favorite ice cream.

On her first visit to his room, it was all she could do to keep from crying. Pallid and weak and badly in need of a shave, Charley lay helpless in his hospital bed. Ominous tubes sprouted from his arms, and the doctors had inserted a pacemaker in his chest. Carolann could barely believe that it was Charley, the same rock 'em, sock 'em, gung-ho cop who had been her partner for the last year and a half.

"Hey, what'sa matter?" whispered Charley, noticing the worried look on her face. "Hey, this is nothin'. I'll be outta here in no time and back on the job, good as new."

But Carolann knew otherwise. At the age of forty-three, Charley's career with the police department was over. Charley himself knew that he would have to put in his retirement papers. He just wasn't ready to admit it.

When the other detectives in the squad came by to visit, they ribbed Charley about engineering the whole thing so he could retire from the job with a juicier pension. By law, cops who suffer heart attacks or other disabling injuries that are job-related can retire at three-quarters pay, rather than at the regular rate of half pay. One of the detectives asked Charley where he bought the heart attack pill. Another accused him of having a sympathetic doctor alter the medical charts.

Carolann kidded him too, but deep down inside she discovered that she could not really accept his illness that lightly. Charley, the rough-and-tumble street cop, had been the only male detective in the office willing to work with her on a full-time basis. After a shaky start, it had blossomed into a remarkably productive partnership, one of the best in the whole squad. Charley had taught her everything he knew, and

Carolann realized that she was a far better cop because of him. She was desperately afraid for Charley. And, knowing that he would no longer be around, she worried for herself, as well.

"Charley," said Carolann during one of her visits to the hospital. "What am I gonna do about all of our cases? I can't work them without you."

But Charley was still determined to keep up the front. "Jesus, Carol, you act like I was sick or something. Listen, I told you, I'll be back on the job in no time."

Carolann could not conceal her concern. "Charley, I'll never be able to find another partner like you."

"That's for sure," laughed Charley. "Nobody else is crazy enough to work with you! You know, partner, I taught you everything you know."

Carolann smiled. "You're absolutely right, Charley—and I still don't know anything."

After a couple of weeks, Charley's condition began to improve. Carolann decided it was safe to leave the city for a few days and go away with some friends for a short vacation in Atlantic City. Charley's heart attack, the endless stall on her promotion, the uncertainty over her future, it was all starting to get to her. She was badly in need of a little relaxation.

One afternoon, as she was lounging by the pool of her hotel in Atlantic City, sipping a cocktail, the loudspeaker began to blare: "Carolann Natale! Carolann Natale! Telephone call! Carolann Natale! Telephone call!"

Fearing the worst, Carolann dashed to a poolside extension.

It was Charley, calling from his hospital bed, and much to Carolann's relief he sounded strong and chipper. The office had been trying frantically to locate Carolann, and they had telephoned Charley, thinking that he might know where she had gone for the weekend.

The reason that they had gone to such lengths to track her down was that there had been an important message from the personnel division in police headquarters. For once, it was good news.

Charley summed it up simply, with his first three words over the phone:

"Hello . . . *Detective* Natale!"

PART THREE

Working The Task Force: Forty-Nine Men—and Carolann

CHAPTER THIRTEEN

Striding purposefully through the gate, the sergeant from the Ninth Precinct Detective Unit slowly scanned the squad room.

"Awright," he announced, "we need guys with mustaches to stand in a lineup. Who's got a mustache?"

He was dismayed to discover that most of the detectives on duty in the Manhattan Detective Area Task Force had clean-shaven upper lips.

"Jesus Christ! You'd think the least the department could do is invest in some fake mustaches so we could run these lineups!"

Disconsolate, the sergeant headed toward the hall, hoping that some of the uniformed police officers in the stationhouse downstairs might show a greater proclivity for facial hair than the detectives upstairs.

It was 5 p.m. and the office of the Manhattan Detective Area Task Force was buzzing like a beehive. While some of the detectives busied themselves with the lineup, others trudged in from old assignments or headed out on new ones. Telephones jangled noisily every few seconds.

Detective Lou Tosi snatched up one of the receivers. "Manhattan Detective Area Task Force, Detective Tosi speaking. May I help you?"

He listened for a moment to the voice on the other end, then shouted out: "Hey, anybody got any messages for Bob McHugh?" McHugh, a senior detective with the squad, was calling in from the field.

Seated at a desk on the other side of the office, Detective Fred McGuire hollered back: "Yeah, tell him to call Paramount Studios! His movie contract is ready!"

Tosi matter-of-factly repeated the message into the receiver. Then, for good measure, he added one of his own. "Oh yeah, call Pot of Gold, too. They want their pot back."

In another corner of the office three detectives clustered around Carolann Natale, watching her unwrap the plastic from the new blue and white jogging suit she had just bought for twelve dollars. "Yep," she explained, "I'm real serious about this. I'm gonna start running in the park near my house."

"You just gonna go jogging?" wondered Detective Steve Del Corso. "Or you gonna sell tickets, too?"

"I'm gonna get back in shape," Carolann announced with determination.

"Then why don't you just stop drinking?" asked Steve, grinning like a Cheshire cat.

"Steve, why don't you just..." Carolann flashed him an ominous smile, but did not bother to finish the sentence.

Just then, Detective Jack Peters walked into the office. Detective Augie Sanchez grabbed him by the elbow. "Hey, Jackie, some guy with a black beard and a long coat was looking for you."

"Hassidim?" asked Peters.

"Who seed 'em?" chorused his partner, Detective Bob Catalano. "I sure didn't seed him."

Deputy Chief Richard Nicastro, the boss of all the Manhattan detectives, walked through the gate, on his way to a meeting with the squad commander, Lieutenant Kluge. Nicastro, a gruff-talking, Colombo-like cop who was genuinely liked and respected by his men, spotted Carolann and made a quick U-turn.

"Where've you been?" he asked. "Haven't seen you around in a while."

"Oh, I've been out sick for a couple of weeks," she answered.

Nicastro gave Carolann a teasing smile. "Pregnant?"

"No, no, gosh no! Flu. Hmmph! Pregnant!"

"Happens to some of the nicest people," said the chief, a gentle twinkle in his eye.

By now, the sergeant from the Ninth Precinct had rounded up four cops, all with full bushy mustaches, to stand in a lineup with a suspect. The suspect, a squat, paunchy man of about thirty with a slack-faced, droopy-eyed expression, had been arrested an hour earlier after he allegedly used a phony police shield to lure a young woman into his car. In the car, he had robbed her of a hundred dollars in cash.

"Probably had more on his mind than just robbery," offered Carolann. "Did they check with the sex crimes squad to see if they've had anyone with a similar m.o.?"

"Hey, who's that?" shouted one of the mustachioed cops in the lineup room as Carolann passed by the door. "Hey, we wanna see what you look like! We heard your voice. You got a sexy voice."

Carolann promptly stepped through the door and into the lineup room. She was wearing a maroon jacket and matching skirt slit fashionably high, a white turtleneck sweater, and black boots.

"Well?" she asked, striking a sultry model's pose, hands on hips. "What's the verdict?"

The cops in the lineup room smiled. "Yeah . . . yeah . . . very nice!"

While the four cops stood off to the side and chatted, the suspect paced back and forth like a caged beast, anxiously waiting for his attorney to arrive. With their full mustaches, the police officers looked like members of the local barbershop quartet. "Best lineup we ever had," glowed the sergeant, clearly pleased with results of his recruiting efforts.

In walked the defendant's lawyer, an oily-looking slickster with regulation pin-striped blue suit, matching vest, and gold-rimmed aviator glasses. For a few moments, he huddled quietly with his client.

"Okay," said the sergeant, slapping his palms together. "Let's get started."

The door to the lineup room was closed and the victim was ushered in to an outer office. She was a petite young woman with the sharply chiseled features of a fashion model. With the sergeant at her side, she glumly walked into an adjoining viewing room and peered through a one-way mirror in the wall at the five men in the lineup. Less than thirty seconds later, the door opened and the young woman was whisked back outside by one of the detectives. The sergeant followed right behind.

"Boom!" he said. "All over! Picked him right out, one, two, three."

The other detectives began the paperwork necessary to charge the suspect with criminal impersonation of a police officer and robbery. The four cops in the lineup wandered out of the room and lit up cigarettes.

One turned to the sergeant. "So what happens now—this case goes down okay and you buy all of us dinner? It doesn't go down okay, you buy his lawyer dinner?"

"Hey, you guys get a pound apiece," assured the sergeant, alluding to the police department's policy of paying five dollars to each person willing to stand in a lineup. The only hitch was that police officers were not eligible for the fees; only civilians could get them. "All you gotta do is turn in your shields," smiled the sergeant.

One of the officers shook his head in mock anguish. "I don't know what happened. When we were inside the lineup room and she was looking at us, we all pointed to *him*," said the cop, gesturing toward another officer in the lineup who was obviously his buddy.

Outside the lineup room, the task force detectives were preoccupied with other matters.

Stan Carr, a black detective, unwrapped the sandwich he had just brought back from the takeout deli around the corner and smacked his lips hungrily. "Hey, this is real soul food I got here: toasted bagel, cream cheese, lox, and a slice of onion."

Returning from police headquarters, where a lie detector test had been given to a female suspect in a stabbing murder, Dominick Bologna reported: "She failed so bad the fuse blew."

Seated at a desk nearby, Leo Rosenthal was still chuckling about the building superintendent the squad had encountered several nights earlier while investigating a double homicide in Harlem. The fellow had been wearing enormous sneakers, completely out of proportion to his diminutive height. The sneakers looked ludicrous, like oversized clown shoes, and nobody could figure out why they were so large. Except for Detective John Jessup who used a bit of common sense and surmised: "Probably because his toenails are eight inches long."

"Hey, you losin' weight, Carl?" asked Detective Al Lopez as he gave Detective Carl Sgrizzi a playful pat on the belly.

"Weight?" laughed Sgrizzi. "I'm losin' money. And I'm losin' hair. And I'm losin' sleep . . . but I sure ain't losin' any weight!"

Detective Jim Coffey whispered to one of the other investigators. "Y'hear about the police dog the department uses to sniff out cocaine?"

"No, what about him?"

Coffey looked one way, then the other. "He's got a $200-a-day habit."

The phone rang, and Carolann reached for one of the extensions. "Manhattan Detective Area Task Force, Detective Natale speaking. May I help you?"

Seconds later, she rolled her eyes upward in an "Oh no!" expression and cupped her hand over the mouthpiece. "Some woman who's supposed to testify in a '75 murder case," Carolann told the other detectives. "She's lookin' for one of the other detectives, but he's not around right now. But, oh boy, is she flying high! Sounds like she's three sheets to the wind already."

Carolann uncupped the mouthpiece. "Well, I'll just have to give him a message. What's your number, dear?"

Just as Carolann hung up, the phone rang again. "Manhattan Detective Area Task Force, Detective Natale speaking. May I help you?"

After listening a moment, Carolann began to bellow at the top of her lungs: "Detective Manero! Anybody seen Jerry Manero?"

Standing barely two feet away, Jerry Manero did not utter a sound. Instead, he arched his eyebrows and flashed Carolann an inquisitive look. Pursing her lips, Carolann gave him a telltale nod, signaling Jerry that the caller was Willie, his most persistent informant.

Six or seven times each day, Willie telephoned the office, always asking to speak with Detective Manero. Sometimes he would provide valuable leads on cases. But more often than not, he would call just to chitchat and pass the time. For some reason, Willie felt compelled to keep Detective Manero posted almost hourly on his whereabouts, be it his home, the local tavern, the pool hall, the barbershop, or the service station where he pumped gas.

Carolann offered Jerry Manero the phone, but Jerry waved it off.

"Sorry, sir," Carolann said into the receiver. "Detective Manero is out in the field right now."

"He's been out in the field so much he oughtta be bringin' Willie flowers," mused Detective John Lafferty.

Having successfully eluded Willie, Jerry Manero turned his attentions to the ally who had just covered for him.

"What are you doin' here so late, Carol?" he wanted to know. "I've never seen you workin' on a Friday night after 6 p.m. I know what *they're* doin' here." Jerry yanked a thumb toward the other detectives in the office. "They're lookin' for night differential. But what are you doin' here?"

"Well, Jerry," began Carolann, "I'm working tonight because I want tomorrow night off. I can't work tomorrow."

"Why not?"

"It'll interfere with my love life."

"Where are you goin' tomorrow night?" asked Jerry. There was something unmistakably impish in his expression.

"Out."

"Out where?"

"Just out."

"Aw, c'mon, Carol. Tell me where. Since when do you and I have any secrets? I'd tell you if I were goin' out. You know that."

Carolann began to laugh. "I have a date with someone special."

Jerry feigned astonishment. "Well *I'm* not goin' out tomorrow night. I'll be home on Staten Island. So who in the world could you be talkin' about?"

Wrinkling up her nose, Carolann answered him ever so teasingly. "None of your business, Jerry."

By 8:30 p.m., all of the other detectives had left the office to go out on cases. The only one left was Carolann. She had decided to stick around because a taxi driver had telephoned earlier in the evening, saying he might stop by to give her some information on a double homicide the squad had been working on. It was a particularly grisly case—two prostitutes whose heads and hands had been chopped off before their corpses were set afire in a midtown motel.

Just as Carolann began to busy herself with some typing, a bald-headed man smoking a pipe shuffled uncertainly into the office, looking like he was lost. "Detective Natale?"

Carolann looked up. "I'm Natale, can I help you? Oh, you must be the taxi driver. Have a seat."

The man studied Carolann with keen interest. "Y'know," he said, "you look just like Shirley Maclaine."

"Thank you," said Carolann, suppressing a smile. "Now, Mr. Miller, can you tell me about the three people you took to the Regency Motel that night?"

Stanley Miller sucked noisily on his pipe, then settled back into the chair near Carolann's desk. He was a slovenly-looking man with a salt-and-pepper beard and long strands of greasy hair hanging limply from the sides of his head just below his bald pate. His ski parka was tattered, his khaki pants were soiled and his yellow jogging shoes looked like they had been deep-fried in mud.

"Well," said Miller, between pipe puffs, "I remember picking up a man and two women and taking them to the hotel."

"Can you describe the people you picked up?" asked Carolann.

Miller snorted loudly, clearing his sinuses. "There was a blonde, a dark-haired girl, and a guy. He was sitting behind me. He had a Southern accent, somewhere from the South."

"Are you sure?"

"Sure I'm sure. I been driving a cab six years now. You can tell these things. You know why I remember this guy? He gave me a twenty-cent tip. A guy goes to a hotel with two girls. He's gonna spend fifty or a hundred dollars on them, right? And he only gives me a twenty-cent tip. Doesn't make sense. I remember things like that. You know, you really do look like Shirley Maclaine; very pretty."

"Thank you, Mr. Miller. Where did you pick these three up?"

Miller tried to rekindle the dying embers in his pipe bowl with a pocket lighter. "Somewhere in the fifties, near the Hilton."

"Do you remember anything they said?"

"Well, they were laughing, just laughing a lot. I remember the blonde was talking to the guy like they were friends."

"What you're telling us is extremely important, Mr. Miller. Please try to remember. What did the man look like?"

"He was nice looking, an average guy. Slim, trim face. Say, you ever get out to Brooklyn, Detective Natale? I live out there and maybe some time—"

Before Miller could complete the invitation, Detective Jim Sullivan walked back into the office and sat down. Carolann filled him in on what she had learned so far and then resumed the Q. and A. "What kind of hair did the man have?"

"You know what?" said Miller, staring hard at Jim Sullivan. "It was like yours, only with a wave in the front. I'm bald, so I remember these things."

Sullivan began to laugh. "Wasn't me. Who asked you to take them to the hotel, the guy or the girls?"

Miller reflected for a moment, biting down on the bit of his pipe. "You know, that's a good question, a very good question . . ."

"What time did you pick them up?" asked Carolann.

"It was in the 10:30 to 11 p.m. range," Miller remembered. "But I'll tell you, the thing that really makes me remember is the tip. He was in a good mood. He was happy. Then he gives me the stiff tip. You know, you could blow a hundred dollars on a horse and not remember it, but something like this, a dollar-eighty or a two-dollar fare and only a twenty-cent tip, you remember it."

"Mr. Miller," said Carolann, "could you go back in your time sheets and see if you have any record of exactly where you picked these people up?"

"Well, I guess I could, but it may take a long time. Might take me a few days to go through them. Unless, maybe you could come over to the garage and give me a hand."

Carolann deftly sidestepped that suggestion. "Suppose we gave you some help—like two men detectives?"

"Why, is it so important to you?"

"Yes, it is. Because if these were the two prostitutes who were murdered and this fellow with the Southern accent was the killer, it would mean a lot."

"Well," said Miller, "I'll tell you the truth, I'm very bad with records. But I'll start going through them to see what I can find. I'll call you tomorrow."

"Here's a number where you can reach me," said Carolann. She wrote the telephone number of the Task Force on a slip of paper.

After Miller left the office, Carolann tried to assess the value of his information. On the one hand, he seemed to offer an intriguing new avenue for the investigation, which so far had been stymied. He might actually have seen the killer and his two victims just before the murders were committed. On the other hand, Carolann was put off by his persistent flattery and his thinly veiled attempts to get better acquainted with her outside the office.

She began to type up a report on the interview. Suddenly, a familiar face was looming over her typewriter. Stanley Miller.

"See that?" he asked indignantly, waving a slip of paper in front of Carolann's face. "I got one." One of the uniformed cops from the stationhouse had tacked a parking ticket to his cab while he was upstairs talking to Carolann.

"Leave that with me, Mr. Miller," Carolann said. "The police department will pay for this one."

(The next day, Stanley Miller would phone Carolann to report that he had been unable to find the time sheets she had requested. But, just so the call would not be a total loss, he would take the occasion to ask her out on a date. Politely, Carolann would decline the invitation.)

About 9:45 p.m., as the other detectives began returning to the office, Carolann and Jim Sullivan broke for dinner at the Greek coffee shop around the corner. Sullivan sampled the broiled sole; Carolann ordered a turkey club sandwich, extra mayonnaise on the side. Over coffee, Sullivan began to reminisce about the night he and another detective had to interrupt their dinner to interrogate a recalcitrant rape suspect.

"I didn't rape that girl," the man had insisted.

One of the detectives tried to bluff him into a confession. "C'mon, we know you did it. Don't give us a hard time."

"But I didn't rape her," the man repeated.

"Listen," interjected the other detective, "we know you did it. You were seen comin' out of her apartment. And what about the neighbors? They told the police they heard screams of terror."

Grinning slyly, the man explained: "Detective, that was my woman and those wasn't screams of terror, those was screams of joy!"

By midnight, only a handful of detectives were still on duty in the task force and all of them, including Carolann, were clustered around the television set in the squad room, engrossed in a rerun of a situation comedy. For the first time all night, the office was totally quiet. So quiet, in fact, that you could hear a pin drop. The detectives were completely absorbed, their eyes glued to the screen.

They were watching "Barney Miller."

CHAPTER FOURTEEN

Carolann had spent another five months with the Manhattan Sex Crimes Squad after winning her gold shield. Charley Valois mended nicely after his heart attack, but in December of 1977 he decided to call it quits. After putting in his retirement papers, he took an executive position in his father's construction business.

His retirement "racket" was a grand gathering, attended by more than one hundred cops who jammed together to hoist their glasses in a boisterous farewell to an irrepressible detective. Carolann helped with the arrangements, and the party was held at Joe and Joe's, the Italian restaurant in the Bronx where she had worked before joining the police force.

For Charley, it was an emotional moment. After all the off-color jokes and the maudlin toasts and the hokey gifts (including a three-foot-tall wood replica of a Keystone Cop), it came time for Charley to address the crowd.

"Speech! Speech!" they clamored.

Charley was almost never at a loss for words. But this time he choked up.

"I love ya's all," he managed to whisper, his voice starting to crack. Then he turned away from the crowd and began dabbing at the corners of his eyes with his massive right hand. For Carolann, it was an emotional moment, too. There would never be another Charley, she knew. As one of the sergeants at the party so aptly described him, "Charley Valois was a diamond in the rough."

Because of her impressive performance with the sex crimes squad—a record due largely to her successful partnership with Charley—Carolann had gone on to work homicide, first with the Ninth Homicide Zone in the Bronx, then with the Fourth Homicide Zone in Manhattan. Two years later, after the police department went through one of its periodic structural shake-ups, the homicide specialty squads in Manhattan were scuttled and a new system was set up. In a throwback to the old days, responsibility for homicides and most other types of investigations was channeled back to the detectives in the local precincts. But to augment and occasionally spearhead major murder investigations, the Detective Bureau decided to field a special corps of supersleuths, ready to rush to the scene of a murder anywhere in Manhattan at a moment's notice.

The Manhattan Detective Area Task Force, as this special corps was known, was one of the most select units in the city, an Ivy League of detective squads. In its ranks were some of the toughest, savviest, most experienced detectives in the entire police department. Many of the detectives were drafted from Carolann's old squad, Fourth Homicide. Joining them was Lieutenant Herman Kluge, the veteran commander of the Fourth who moved over to take the helm of the task force.

In racial and ethnic makeup, the task force was as rich and varied as the turf it policed, a miniature melting pot of white cops, black cops, and Hispanic cops. There were Irish detectives, Italian detectives, and Jewish detectives, as well as detectives whose ancestry was German, English, Scottish, and even American Indian.

All in all, the task force had fifty investigators.

Forty-nine men.
And one woman: Carolann Natale.

On New Year's Day, not long after the task force commenced operations, a forty-two-year-old woman was found strangled inside her apartment, a stocking knotted tightly around her neck. The detectives from the First Precinct in Lower Manhattan had caught the case and gotten the first glimpse of the body. But the detectives from the task force were asked to lend a hand. A few nights after the murder, Carolann and Detective Leo Rosenthal decided to visit the First Precinct detectives for a briefing.

Leo already had familiarized himself with some of the details of the case. The problem up to that point, he explained, was a scarcity of witnesses. "It was a holiday," he told Carolann as they drove downtown together. "You know how everybody gets on a holiday. Nursing hangovers. Nobody saw nothing."

Leo was the kind of detective who wore a perpetual look of bemusement. After years of investigating homicides, absolutely nothing surprised him.

Tucked among a cluster of dingy warehouses and showrooms in Lower Manhattan, the First Precinct stationhouse was a turn-of-the-century relic painted in drab greens and blues, splotched with plaster patches and adorned with creaking metal chandeliers from another era. The stationhouse mascot, a huge German sherpherd with sad, brown eyes, lay sprawled in the entrance, head tucked between its two front paws. Carolann and Leo stepped around gingerly, careful not to antagonize him.

Upstairs, in a musty green office, three detectives were sipping coffee and doing paperwork. One sat with his feet propped on a typewriter, drawing slowly and sensuously on a filter-tipped cigarette.

A handsome man in his mid-thirties, he had the crisp, contemporary look of a movie producer or a record company mogul: long, dark hair falling well below the ears but stylishly shaped, full mustache, gold-rimmed aviator glasses, blue three-piece suit, starched white shirt with gold cufflinks, expensive silk tie knotted in perfect symmetry at the collar.

Detective Gerry Brigante exchanged greetings with Leo. Leo introduced Carolann. Brigante smiled, surprised and delighted to discover that the department had such good-looking women detectives. Then, opening a manila folder, he began to give Leo and Carolann a rundown on the case.

"My theory is that whoever killed this woman knew her," he began. There was a tough-guy, Bogart-like inflection to Brigante's speech, but he chose his words with precision and expressed himself articulately.

"There was a dog in the apartment and that dog was vicious. When we arrived, he did everything but kill us. He wanted to eat us. It must have been somebody she knew or the dog would never have let him near her. At the scene, there was a coffee cup lying on the table. The killer went into the bathroom, took a stocking out of the hamper, and then strangled her. Whoever it was also took several hundred dollars' worth of coins. That was the only thing missing."

Carolann wondered about possible suspects. "There was a stepdaughter, wasn't there?" she remembered. "What was the situation between the dead woman and her stepdaughter?"

"They were only ten years apart," said Brigante. "The stepdaughter had an ex-husband who she was still seeing from time to time. My guess is that hubby came over and he wanted to play with Mamma. But Mamma said no go. So he strangled her."

Leo had been listening quietly to Brigante's theory. "Do we know the name of the ex-husband?" he asked.

Brigante glanced at the case folder. "Edwards. Jimmy Edwards."

"Holy Jeez!" exclaimed Leo. "I know him. He's bad news. Did three years in the can for manslaughter. He's a big guy, too. He could probably have picked this woman up and hung her with one hand. Mark that down. Let's find out about the relationship between Edwards and the deceased. That whole family is bad, all those Edwards boys. We locked 'em up when I was in First Homicide."

"How come you just didn't shoot 'em?" asked Brigante.

"We came close a couple of times," laughed Leo.

"Close don't count," said Carolann drily.

Brigante continued with his analysis: "This girl, the stepdaughter, she's a junkie. She was married a second time, to a junkie burglar who fell off a fire escape with all the loot and went DOA. A year later, her original husband, this Edwards guy, comes back and he did time for manslaughter. Now the mother goes DOA. There's too much death here, too much coincidence."

Poking his hand in the air, in search of an elusive target, Brigante surmised: "It's gotta be there somewhere. I said from the very first day it was the son-in-law. He wanted to mess with Mamma, but she decided to squeal. So he strangled her."

Something Brigante had mentioned earlier was gnawing at Carolann. Something about a dog in the apartment.

"Timewise, when was the victim last seen walking the dog?" she asked Brigante.

"Ten, ten-thirty."

"Then how come the dog didn't bark when he was inside the apartment?" Carolann wondered.

Detectives were always curious about barking dogs. In murder case after murder case, the point was one of the first to come up. The line of reasoning behind it was really quite simple: If a dog was present at the time of the murder, it probably saw the killer. But if the dog did not bark, then it did not react to the killer as an intruder. That meant that the killer might have been there before. Which, in turn, suggested that the killer was no stranger to the victim. Operating on the assumption that the killer was known to the victim, the detectives could substantially narrow down the list of suspects.

Brigante re-examined the "barking dog" theory, zeroing in on possible flaws.

"We're all presuming the dog didn't bark," he began. "But the people in the back of the building were hard of hearing. We don't know for sure that the dog didn't bark. Who says the dog didn't bark? The dog's food and drinking dish were in another room. The victim's son showed me his scratch marks on the louvered doors. The dog knew how to open those doors to get into the living room. He was sitting there, by the body, when we arrived. Wouldn't let anybody near it. Still, he must have let somebody in that apartment. Somebody who knew that woman."

Leo picked up on Brigante's train of thought and began to

flesh it out. "Maybe the killer had just woken up. That's why the coffee cup was still there, on the table. Then, maybe he's feeling his oats . . . but the woman is not in the mood. So he kills her."

"They must have done something," agreed Brigante. "Doesn't the M.E. check for any signs of sex acts when there's a dead body?"

"Not unless there's evidence of a rape," said Carolann, remembering her days as a sex crimes investigator. "How about the victim's bed? Was it made? Was it rumpled?"

"Rumpled," said Brigante.

Just then, a gray and white tomcat tiptoed into the squad office and darted under one of the desks. Carolann began to make kissing noises, tyring to attract the cat's attention. But the cat was playing hard to get.

"Chases the mice up here," explained one of the other detectives. With the dog downstairs and the cat upstairs, the First Precinct was beginning to resemble an animal shelter.

The detectives resumed their analysis of the murder. Just for argument's sake, they began to bat around other possibilities besides a lover's quarrel. "That stocking was knotted," said Brigante. "What if she just hung herself and then the father cut her down when he found the body?"

"No way," said Leo. "You could tell because of the ligature." Drawing his hands into a semi-circle around his own neck to illustrate, Leo explained: "If the marks on the neck go straight up, the victim has been hanging. Suicide. If the marks go straight back, it means the victim was garroted. Homicide."

"Maybe a woman did it," theorized Carolann. "Maybe a woman stayed over and used a stocking to kill her. By the way, how'd the son take the news of his mother's death?"

"Cold as ice," sniffed Brigante. "Cold as ice."

"And the parents?"

"They took it kinda hard."

The victim had earned the reputation of being an easy pickup, especially for younger men. "Where'd she meet all her lovers?" wondered Carolann.

"Locally, in bars in the neighborhood," replied Brigante. "She was forty-two. They were twenty-six, twenty-nine . . ."

Brigante seemed impressed by Carolann's questions. Obviously, she knew what she was doing; something most cops considered rare among their female colleagues.

When Leo began to thumb through "the fives," the original reports typed up by the detectives at the scene of the murder, Brigante took the occasion to question Carolann about her experiences in the ranks. He wondered if she had encountered obstacles in making it to detective.

Carolann spoke candidly. "If you're doing the job, catching the cases, carrying your weight, then you should get the money," she told him. "You feel like you're a second-class citizen when you don't have the shield. This male-female business, it's nonsense. If you feel that you're qualified to do the job, then you should do it."

"I don't know about that," Brigante said, twirling his cigarette lighter with his fingers as he spoke. "I love women in the department. I love women in general. The greatest thing since animal crackers. As far as women partners, there's even a few of 'em... I couldn't make a pimple on their rear ends. Hey, they're beautiful. First-rate cops.

"But physically speaking, you take a young woman and you put her in a squad... In my male egotism, I would feel responsible for you. I couldn't let anything happen to you. I always had that feeling of responsibility. But I admit, that was the way I was brought up. An Italian family. I had sisters. You're taught to take care of them. I know you want to be accepted. But you don't want to be hurt."

"Listen," said Carolann, "I had a male partner in sex crimes. He didn't worry about me taking care of myself. One time, he left me flat on my face on 125th Street in Harlem to go chasing after some perp. He didn't stop to pick me up. I think it's a simple thing, this partner business. If it's a male and he feels he can handle anything alone, then he can handle a female partner. But if he always needs a partner to do his job, if he can't do anything at all without a partner—then he's gonna want another male."

Brigante was fascinated. "You know," he said, "I never thought about it like that. That's very interesting. I may have to rethink the whole situation."

By the time Leo had finished reading all the reports, it was nearly ten o'clock, so the two task force detectives decided to break for dinner. After bidding goodbye to Brigante, they drove to Chinatown.

Not only was Leo Rosenthal the task force's expert on Chinese youth gangs; he was also the expert on Chinese restaurants. With Leo doing the ordering at the Hong Ying Rice Shoppe, a basement eatery on Mott Street, Carolann sampled a savory assortment of barbecued steak cubes wrapped in bacon strips, clams in black bean sauce, sauteed pork and scallops and yung chow fried rice, all for about fifteen dollars.

After eating, the detectives drove back to Little Italy to look for witnesses in the five-story tenement where the woman had been strangled. Checking the mailboxes, Leo discovered that the victim had lived on the fifth floor. Carolann headed up the stairs. Leo was right behind.

At the third-floor landing, he stopped to catch his breath and utter a familiar detective gripe: "Why is it that nothing happens on the first floor?"

There were four apartments on the fifth floor. The detectives rang each bell. No one answered.

"Another thing about the top floor," sighed Carolann, now painfully aware of that extra helping of pork and scallops. "Once you get up there, they're never home."

The Little Italy case was put on the back burner when the task force found itself swamped by torso murders.

The detectives were already at their wits' end with the slayings of the two young prostitutes whose heads and hands were severed before their corpses were set on fire in a midtown motel. Like many investigations, this one had been marked by plenty of promising leads, most of which fizzled into dead ends. A case in point: the scruffy-looking taxi driver who had visited Carolann in the office and had related his vivid tale of three suspicious passengers, two girls and their cheap-tipping companion. This investigation was further stymied by the inability of the police to immediately identify the victims. With their heads gone, there was no way of knowing what they looked like. And with their hands missing too, it was impossible to run a check on their fingerprints.

Not long after the murders of the prostitutes, the task force was drawn into still another torso slaying, this one an old case. A man who had stabbed his mother twenty-four times with a butcher knife and then hacked off her head waltzed past his guards at a local mental hospital, made his way into Manhattan, and simply disappeared. Eight years earlier, Richard Granger had been acquitted of murder charges by reason of insanity. But now he was on the loose again and still considered dangerous. A citywide manhunt was launched. The detectives of the task force were recruited for the search.

One night, as Carolann and several dozen other detectives crowded around the desk in his glass-enclosed office, Lieutenant Kluge held a briefing on the two torso cases.

He began with the "double." A car had been spotted outside the motel where the prostitutes were murdered. Green Camaro, New Jersey plates. It could have belonged to the killer. The lieutenant wanted to circulate fliers with a description among the New Jersey police.

"How come we just don't broadcast a description of the car over the radio?" wondered one of the detectives.

"For a good reason," replied the lieutenant. "If you got a green Camaro with Jersey plates and you're happily married and we put that description over the air—hey, that guy may come home and walk into a rolling pin because his wife thinks he's been up to no good."

Kluge pulled a large map of New Jersey out of his top drawer.

"Now, here's the way we're gonna work it. Each of you will take a different town in Jersey and go talk to the local police. Give them these fliers. We gotta do this like it's the domino theory. Start off with a twenty-five mile radius. Then work out to a fifty-mile radius. We'll do it so we get ripple effect."

The lieutenant started to unfurl the map, only to discover that it was riddled with pinpricks and small rips. At the center, just about where the capital of Trenton should have been, there was a gaping hole, big enough to stick two fingers through.

"Jeez, how'd that happen?" Kluge wondered. Befuddled, he held the map up to the light for a closer look.

"The mouse got it!" laughed Carolann.

"Looks like a dart board," said Augie Sanchez.

"Hmmph!" muttered Kluge. "Some way to conduct an investigation. Guess the kids got into this. Either that, or my wife was using this to stick pins in."

"Or strain the spaghetti," suggested Pat Papagallo.

"All right," said the lieutenant, sliding the tattered map back in his desk. "We'll get a new map. In any case, you all know what you have to do. Now, what about our missing mental patient who walked out of the hospital? There's a strong possibility he's in the drink."

"Well, it's winter now and the water's still cold," said Sgt. Matt McAleary, a tall, strapping supervisor with wavy blond hair. "We may have to wait until spring, when the water warms up and the body gases expand. Then it'll float to the surface."

Augie Sanchez came up with a novel suggestion. "Why don't we just heat the water?" he asked, breaking into a grin.

Peering over the tops of his bifocals, Kluge rekindled a thumb-sized length of cigar. "What else do we have on this guy?" he asked McAleary.

McAleary pulled a small notepad from his inside jacket pocket. He began flipping the pages. "He did a stickup a few years back with a shotgun. Walked in, followed the clerk into the store and kept asking, 'Where's the money?' The clerk leads him deeper and deeper into the store, then he points at the register. Granger tries to open the register, but he can't. By then, the police have arrived and they arrest him. Later, his lawyer asks him, 'How come you couldn't open the register?' Granger tells him: 'I thought it was the adding machine.'"

"What about the murder of the mother?" asked the lieutenant, working hard to keep the cigar nub from dying out.

"Used to masturbate in front of her. Stabbed her in the back before he cut her head off. He couldn't face her. If you ever find him, he won't be able to face you either. He'll turn away. The other thing is that he's got plenty of money to go traveling. He had $2,600 saved up and the hospital put it aside for him. Also, Social Security had made a $10,000 settlement with him and they paid him off in a lump sum. That's how he got the money to pay his lawyer for his trial."

"Ten thousand dollars!" Detective John Lafferty sighed. "This guy has more money in the bank than I saved in nineteen years on the job. One doctor says he's a model patient. Another says he's dangerous. Meanwhile, he just walks out of the hospital, gets on the D train, starts talking to the walls and the doors. Next thing you know, he'll be lopping off a few more heads."

The very next day, the task force got word that Richard Granger, the escaped mental patient, had telephoned the mental hospital and told his doctors that he wanted to return. Supposedly, he had made the call from a telephone booth on Manhattan's West Side. The detectives dashed for their cars and headed for the West Side, hoping to spot Granger on the street before he changed his mind about surrendering.

Carolann rode with Jerry Manero and Marty Martinez. Marty took the wheel.

"Okay, Carol, here's what we're gonna do if we spot Richard on the street," said Jerry, talking at his usual staccato clip, a mile a minute. Sometimes, Jerry sounded as though he had been vaccinated with a Victrola needle. "I'll talk to him first and ask him to come back. If he says no, I'll say 'Fine, you stay here. I'll leave. Carol will talk to you.'"

"Thanks a lot!" laughed Carolann, remembering how Granger's last female victim had fared.

Just as the detectives neared Twenty-third Street and Eighth Avenue, their car stalled and lurched to a halt.

"Hang on, Richard!" Jerry shouted in mock supplication. "We're tryin' to get there. We'll be about twenty minutes late."

"This must be the chase car," said Carolann.

"This car..." moaned Jerry. "By the time we get it to Philadelphia, it'll be warmed up."

Marty turned the key in the ignition and pumped the gas pedal and the car engine sputtered back to life. Much relieved, the three detectives headed north along Eighth Avenue, scanning the sidewalks for the missing mental patient. Marty pulled a copy of the wanted poster from his pocket. "Look at that face. He's got a baby face. If you see some guy just standing around and looking up at the sky, that's him."

"Let's head for Times Square," said Jerry. "If I were a mental case, that's where I'd go."

"I got news for you, Jerry," said Carolann. "You *are* a mental case."

"I love you, too, Carol."

At four o'clock in the afternoon, Times Square was teeming with human riffraff, whores and junkies and winos and con artists and pickpockets, loitering under the theater marquees or in front of the porno shops and fast-food joints. Jerry studied them with disgust. "Look at all these guys. Somebody should come down here with a big net. Scoop 'em all up and tow 'em out to sea, out beyond the two-hundred-mile limit. Stop the car, Marty."

At the corner of Forty-second Street and Broadway, Jerry hopped out and ran to a pay telephone. A moment later, he was back in the front seat.

"Good news," he announced. "I just called the office. Richard is back. He just walked into the mental hospital by himself."

"Nice goin', Jerry," said Carolann. "You cracked another one."

Jerry clucked his tongue and wiped a hand across his brow, signaling both exhaustion and relief. "Like I always say, Carol. Perseverance pays off in these big cases."

Some weeks later, the task force returned to the Times Square area on still a third torso murder. A dismembered body was discovered in a shopping cart on West Forty-eighth Street, minus the head, arms and lower parts of the legs. By following a trail of blood along the sidewalk, sanitation men and police officers found the missing limbs, stuffed like leftovers in plastic bags, around the corner on West Forty-seventh Street.

Unlike the unsolved "double," the Forty-eighth Street torso murder was open and shut. A grounder. The victim was quickly identified as a sixty-three-year-old man who owned a garment factory in Chinatown. Detectives from the local precinct learned that he had been paying regular visits to a nineteen-year-old topless dancer, a suspected prostitute. They arrested the dancer's boyfriend, a performer in live sex shows, and charged him with the murder. The dancer and another man were taken into custody as material witnesses.

The following night, detectives from the task force were

assigned to scoop up stand-ins for lineups. Their objective: Find men who resembled both the suspected killer and the man who was being held as a material witness. One had to be a tall, skinny black with a bushy afro; the other, a short black in his early twenties with close-cropped hair.

Cruising along Eighth Avenue in a navy blue Plymouth, Carolann found herself once again surveying the Times Square regulars. This time, Detective Jim Sullivan was with her. "Let's try to get them in a group," she suggested to Jim. "They'll be more apt to come back to the stationhouse for a lineup if they're with some friends."

Turning down a side street, Jim Sullivan spotted four black men standing in a circle, sucking on pint bottles concealed in paper bags. He rolled down his window. "Hey, wanna make some money?"

One of the men stumbled toward the car.

"We need some guys to come back to the stationhouse," Sullivan told him. "We're detectives."

"How many you need?" asked the man.

"We can take four or five," said Jim. "For a lineup."

The man walked back toward his friends and they huddled for a moment, talking strategy. Suddenly, one broke ranks and bellowed out: "Shee-*it!* I ain't goin' with no damned cops!" Waving his bottle in the air, he began bobbing and weaving up the street.

His departure precipitated an outbreak of cold feet. The other three men quickly followed his example and scattered in different directions.

"Oh, Jeez," said Carolann disgustedly. "We don't need this. Those guys are all high as kites. Let's go." Jim hit the accelerator.

At Forty-second Street and Eighth Avenue, milling in front of a peep show, were four more young black men, all fairly short. Carolann rolled down her window and signaled to the one who looked to be the leader.

"Yo!" she shouted.

The young man glanced at the car and snickered. An unmarked squad car was about as hard to recognize as an ostrich with its head stuck in the ground. The young man had made them for cops almost instantly. Undaunted, he sauntered toward them.

Jim Sullivan gave the sales pitch. "Hey, you wanna make some fast money?"

"What do I have to do?" asked the young man.

"Just stand in a lineup. It'll take you five minutes."

"How much?"

"Five bucks for five minutes."

"I don't know, man . . . I got some friends here with me."

Jim Sullivan glanced past him. "How many friends you got?"

"There's three guys over there."

"Well," said Jim, "it's worth five bucks apiece to them, too."

The young man trotted back toward his friends. All at once, they came charging forward, falling all over each other to squeeze into the back seat of the squad car. A fifth man, clutching a can of Budweiser, tried to muscle in. But the group leader blocked his path. "Nah, nah," he told the interloper. "We got four. That's enough, man."

After Carolann and Jim Sullivan had deposited the first batch of stand-ins at the Midtown North precinct on West Fifty-fourth Street, they looped back to Times Square again to look for a second batch. Like seasoned anglers who know where the fish are biting, the two detectives made a beeline for the corner of Forty-second Street and Eighth Avenue. A tall, young black man with a hooded parka was leaning against a corner, smoking a cigarette.

"Yo!" shouted Carolann, waving him toward the car. He stepped up to the window. "We're detectives."

"Yeah," he smiled. "I knew that."

"How'd you like to earn five dollars?"

"For what?"

"Five minutes of your time. Just stand in a lineup."

"Oh, I done that before. But it took three or four hours. I ain't got that kinda time."

"No, no," assured Carolann. "It's not gonna take that long. Five minutes, that's all. We'll take you there, we'll bring you back."

"Okay."

"Hey, by the way," said Carolann. "You got any friends around?"

"Yeah," said the young man. "Up by the movie." He pointed to a cluster of young men in front of a marquee. The feature that night was *Oriental Lust: A New Slant on Sex*.

"Think your friends might wanna come, too?" asked Carolann.

"Sure," said the young man. He walked back toward the group. A moment later, four young men, all fairly tall, were piling into the back seat of the squad car.

"How much we gonna get for this?" asked one of the stand-ins.

"Five apiece," said Jim Sullivan, heading the car back uptown, toward the stationhouse.

"Aw-*right!*" said the young man, delighted with the terms.

"We know 'bout lineups," said one of the others. "But what'd this dude do?"

"A homicide," answered Carolann.

"Is he a brother?" asked another young man.

"Shit, man," muttered his friend. "Course he's a brother. What you think they'd be wantin' with us if he weren't no brother?"

As Carolann and Jim Sullivan sat quietly in the front seat, absorbed, the four young men in the rear carried on an animated discussion about crime and violence in the big city.

"A homicide!" exclaimed one. "Whoa boy!"

"Man," said another, "there's all kindsa weird shit goin' on round here. Look at them two hookers got their heads and hands cut off."

Carolann and Jim exchanged glances, but said nothing.

"Yeah," continued one of the young men. "I know why those girls got their hands cut off. They be dippin' into too many of the johns' pockets."

"Probably the same john," suggested his friend.

"Musta been an awful lot of blood over there."

"I'll bet it smelled bad, too. I know what dead bodies smell like."

"How you know that?"

"I worked out in Potter's Field once. I put some of 'em in the ground. But seven dollars an hour ain't enough to pay for that smell. They used to have the bodies piled up and we'd have to lay 'em out flat and put 'em in boxes. But I didn't do that for very long. I couldn't take the smell, man."

When the two detectives returned with the four young men to the Midtown North Precinct, it looked like the start of a class reunion. The four short stand-ins and the four tall stand-ins, all acquaintances from Forty-second Street, greeted each other like long-lost relatives, palms slapping palms loudly.

"Well, fancy seein' you here!"

"Hey, brother, what's happenin'?"

With a full cast of stand-ins now assembled and the lineups ready to proceed, Carolann and Jim decided to call it a night. Skirting the television camera crews who were waiting outside for a press conference, they returned to their car and drove back downtown to the task force office on East Twenty-first Street.

Around midnight, just as Carolann was about to start typing up her report, a call came in.

"Your son," said the detective who answered the phone.

Carolann reached anxiously for the receiver, transformed instantaneously from thick-skinned detective to concerned parent.

Because of an injury Johnny had suffered while playing football, his knee had been placed in a cast. Surgery to repair the torn ligaments was imminent, and Carolann was worried sick. She was on the phone for about twenty minutes.

"Johnny," she said, "would you please take care of yourself? You know how accident-prone you are. Just be careful, will you? Yes... Yes... okay. What are you gonna get for your birthday? Did you get my card? I put a little something in it for you. Will you write to me? Please? Okay... I love you, too. Take care. Goodbye."

Carolann hung up the receiver. Looking up at the other detectives, she sighed.

"My baby! I can't believe it. He's gonna be twenty years old. He's determined to finish college. He wants time for his girlfriends. He's all grown up now. So he goes and pulls ligaments in his knee and they put him in a cast.

"Now he tells me he wants to go hang-gliding. He's gonna drive me crazy."

CHAPTER FIFTEEN

Carolann had always felt an extra measure of motherly concern for her son, ever since his near-fatal illness in infancy. With his devil-may-care friskiness, Johnny seemed to have a propensity for injuries. Brenda Lee had always been perfectly able to take care of herself, but Johnny, for some reason, was accident-prone. The banged-up knee was only the latest of his many mishaps.

As a child, while playing, he had inadvertently tumbled through a plate-glass door and slashed his face so badly that fifteen stitches were required to close the wound, which came perilously close to one of his eyes. Carolann was called to the hospital from her policewoman's post when it happened. Later, when Johnny was in his teens, an accident on a camping trip had nearly cost him his life. He was sitting around a campfire one night when a hot cinderblock exploded, showering him with burning embers. Suddenly, his clothes were on fire. One of his friends was quick-witted enough to hurl him to the ground and roll him back and forth until the flames were snuffed out. But not before they left him with second- and third-degree burns over his back, neck, face, and arm. Johnny spent three weeks in a hospital recuperating.

Gone from home for nearly a year now, stationed at a Naval base three-thousand miles away, Johnny was constantly on his mother's mind. She worried about him for days on end and lived for his long-distance telephone calls, anxious to hear the sound of his voice and reassure herself that he was happy and active—and still in one piece.

When not worrying, Carolann behaved like most other mothers, unabashedly singing her son's praises. "Johnny wants to take the ROTC test and finish college," she would tell her friends. "He's really got his feet solid on the ground now. He's taking a lot of math courses to help pass the entrance exam. If he passes the exam, he can come home to go to college. He can live with me. He'll be good company for me.

"He's got that personality. He loves old people. He loves children. He can talk to anyone. That kid's gotta succeed in life, he's got everything goin' for him. He's a character, he really is. I'm very proud of him. I really miss him."

Carolann had scheduled a two-week vacation for the fall of 1980, intending to visit Johnny out on the West Coast. All year long, she talked of the plans they had made, all the things they would do when they were together—a tour around the base to meet his friends and commanding officers, a sailboat outing (both mother and son were accomplished helmsmen), a visit to San Francisco's Chinatown, a drive down the picturesque coastal highway, a reunion with one of Johnny's cousins who was stationed at an Air Force base in California.

Then, a week before Carolann was due to depart, came the bad news. Johnny told her about it one night on the phone.

Because of the injury to his knee and the surgery he had had to undergo, he was now obliged by the Navy to do ninety days of disability duty. That meant ninety days of work in the base cafeteria, preparing meals. His day would begin at 4 a.m. and end at 6 p.m. He was still attending college classes three nights a week. But, because of regulations, he would be unable to take any leaves at all during the ninety days. And he would have no time whatsoever to spend with Carolann.

Carolann was crushed. But she had to agree with Johnny that it would be best for her to call off the trip. Now, the earliest she could possibly see him would be Christmas. But even that was not a certainty. For days she moped around the task force office, sullen and moody.

"Today's my turn to be depressed," she told her partners, Dominick Bologna and Carl Sgrizzi, one morning. "You two have to cheer me up."

"Oh?" said Dominick. "So you're the only one who can be upset today? We can't be upset?"

"Nope," said Carolann. "Not today. You have to cheer me up."

Dominick decided to try a little pep talk to perk her spirits. Imitating a straight-by-the-book superior officer, he told Carolann: "You know, Detective Natale, you're not supposed to bring your problems to work with you. You're supposed to leave your problems at home."

And, just for a moment, it worked. "Oh, Dominick," called Carolann, waiting for him to look up from some paperwork.

As soon as he did, she playfully thumbed her nose at him.

With the trip to California off, Carolann tried to console herself with one-day outings, family get-togethers, and weekend trips. In the company of two girlfriends, she visited some friends who had a beach house on Fire Island. They arrived early, armed with swimsuits, umbrellas, blankets, and air mattresses, and enough food and drink to feed a whole platoon of cops. To mark the occasion, Carolann wore a blue T-shirt emblazoned with a cherubic likeness of Porky Pig in a policeman's uniform. Porky's printed message, given with a characteristic stutter, was: "Up ag-ag-against th-th-the wall, M-Mother f-f-fu-fu . . ."

While Carolann enjoyed visiting friends, her idea of a really good time was to entertain at home. With its sweeping view of Long Island Sound, her apartment was ideal for parties and cookouts. When the weather was fair and the wind cooperated, she would take guests sailing in the little nine-foot, 110-pound dinghy she kept in the backyard. Afterwards, there was usually a barbecue. One July Fourth she played host to thirty friends and relatives for a feast that included barbecued chicken, hot dogs, hamburgers, spare ribs, sausages and peppers, corn on the cob, bean salad, piña coladas, and plenty of wine. For dessert, there were fresh blueberries with cream and Cointreau.

One thing that Carolann generally avoided doing was socializing with the male detectives after hours. She loved going to "rackets," the police parties that were regularly thrown for retirements and promotions, but hanging out in bars was not her style. It made her uncomfortable. She perceived a bar as "a man's world," a setting where she would be "out of place." The only bar that she had ever frequented was Joe and Joe's in the Bronx, and that was because she had worked there.

Romantically speaking, Carolann was still of a mind to shun heavy attachments. During her first year with the task force, she dated different people, including a lawyer and a retired detective, but her basic outlook, now that both children had moved out of the house, was to avoid commitments and "play the field awhile."

Marriage definitely did not appeal to her. At times, she thought it might be better just to live with someone. Times were changing and such arrangements were common and accepted among couples. Nevertheless, for Carolann a decision to cohabit casually would never be an easy one. Not that she was a prude, but neither did she see herself as a totally liberated woman. Carolann's dilemma was that she was neither an "old-fashioned girl" nor a "modern girl," but a breed in between. Or, as she herself liked to phrase it, an "old-fashioned modern."

Sometimes she would discuss her attitudes on marriage with two of her partners in the task force, Carl Sgrizzi and Dominick Bologna.

Carl was a sardonic, street-smart veteran, one of the best joke-tellers in the entire squad. Partial to dark, conservative suits and white shirts, he had a strong nose and jaw and fine gray hair, a combination of attire and physical characteristics which gave him the bearing of a judge or a Park Avenue physician. Dominick, taller and a few years younger, had wavy black hair with a distinguished ripple of gray just above the

sideburns. A more colorful dresser than Carl, Dominick preferred striped or checked jackets, bright shirts, and bold ties.

While Carl was terse, incisive, and to the point, Dominick
was methodical and analytical. Having earned college degrees
in both the social sciences and police science, he was forever
intrigued by what made people tick, the psychology behind
their actions, and he delighted in playing the devil's advocate
in discussions about court decisions or police procedures or a
suspect's motives, just to see what kind of reactions he might
provoke.

Both Carl and Dominick were family men, devoted husbands, loving fathers, and firm believers in the institution of
marriage. On that subject, however, Carolann delighted in en-
gaging them in friendly arguments.

One night, as the three detectives were driving up to the
West Side on a case, they became embroiled in a spirited debate
on a subject of crucial importance: the best recipe for spaghetti
sauce. Carolann was firmly convinced that, in this particular
department, she had no competitors.

"But do you brown your meatballs and your pork in one
pan and cook your sauce in another pan?" asked Dominick,
who was equally certain that his sauce was the best to ever
grace a plate of pasta.

Carolann turned up her nose. "Ahhhhh, that's crazy! You
cook 'em both together."

"What do you know?" teased Dominick. "You're Polish."

"Half Polish," corrected Carolann. "And half Italian."

Dominick waved her off. "Listen, listen to me—here's the
way you should make your sauce," and he proceeded to give
her a blow-by-blow rundown of the requisite ingredients and
cooking techniques.

All the talk about food prompted Carl to chime in with an
endorsement for his own wife, whom he lauded as "an excellent
cook."

"Poor woman," sniffed Carolann. "Always slaving over a
hot stove." Carl laughed out loud.

"I help my wife," interjected Dominick. "Whenever I can."

That was reason enough for Carolann to take up the cause
of oppressed housewives. "Ohhhhhhhhh! But she has to clean

the house, whether she feels like it or not. She has to cook the supper, whether she feels like it or not. Can you imagine me, at my age, with the way I've lived my life, as independent as I've been, taking on the responsibility of a husband? I'd have to cook, I'd have to clean, I'd have to devote myself to another person. It would be like taking care of a child."

Dominick tried to reason with her. "The trouble with you, Carol, is that you just haven't met the right man yet. If you met the right man, you'd be happy to do these things."

"Yeah, sure," scoffed Carolann, hardly sounding convinced.

Carl, who was behind the wheel of the car, offered a slightly different assessment on Carolann's love life. "You know what your problem is?" he began. "You should have married a *real* Italian. He'd make you toe the line. Ever hear the expression, 'You'd walk with both feet in one shoe.'?"

Carolann pondered the remark for a few seconds. "What does that mean—that he'd keep me hoppin'?"

Carl merely glanced into the rearview mirror so Carolann could see the expression on his face. He looked like the cat who had swallowed the canary.

"Oh, yeah?" snapped Carolann, half-giggling herself now. "Listen, if I was married to either one of you, I could have straightened you *both* out!"

With that, all three detectives began to laugh.

CHAPTER SIXTEEN

Lieutenant Kluge glanced at his watch. "All right, let's get over there. We don't want to be late."

Adjusting the brim of his tan fedora, Kluge stuffed both hands into the pockets of his overcoat and walked purposefully down the stationhouse steps, toward a waiting squad car. Carolann and half a dozen other detectives followed closely behind.

It was cold, so very cold, on that first morning in February as the detectives made their way through the morning traffic, down Manhattan's East Side Drive and into Brooklyn by way of the tunnel that runs under the East River. Puddles of water had frozen into slick patches of ice on the city's streets and car engines spewed off clouds of white vapor.

Inside their squad car, Carolann, Kluge and Detective Bennie Leotta reminisced about their early years on the job. The bizarre cases. The wily criminals. The cantankerous bosses.

The zany partners. They chatted about friends and families, wives and husbands, vacations and retirement parties, weddings and funerals.

But it was all a facade. Something to mask their real feelings. For deep down inside, under all the chitchat, the three detectives felt angry and hurt and bitter. And unspeakably sad.

As the car pulled up to the red brick church, Carolann stepped outside and took her place with the others. An ice-edged wind lashed meanly at her face, but she stood there silently, beneath a blazing blue sky, transfixed by the spectacle before her eyes.

Around her was a sea of blue, row upon row of police officers standing in ranks as far as the eye could see. Young patrolmen in their pressed navy blue uniforms and dress white gloves. Detectives and older commanding officers in trench coats, their graying hair tousled by the wind. City policemen and transit policemen. Housing cops and auxiliary cops. FBI agents and state troopers and sheriffs' deputies. Policemen from other counties and other states and even from other countries. All told, more than five thousand peace officers stood silently outside that red brick church in Brooklyn, shivering in the cold.

And then it began.

A drum major raised an enormous scepter high into the air, its polished metal surface gleaming in the bright sun. For a few seconds, he held it aloft, waiting until all heads turned to watch. Then he brought his arm down sharply. At the signal, the muffled thumping of a dozen drums began to echo through the street. The thumping grew louder, then closer, moving slowly and inexorably toward the church.

Grimly, Carolann pulled her gold detective's shield from her purse and pinned it to the outside of her overcoat. Like the other cops who were there that day, she had stretched a black band across the face of the badge.

A uniformed sergeant standing a few feet away raised a megaphone to his lips. "Ten-*Shun!*" he barked, and the army of uniformed cops went rigid.

Down the street, step by deliberate step, marched the bag-pipers, huge, beefy men in black kilts and black feather bonnets. The wind had turned their cheeks ruddy and raw, but not once did they break stride with the cadence of the drums. Next came the drummers. Perched on their heads were Balmorals, the flat, brimless caps traditional to Scotland. Slowly and mechanically, they pounded their drums, each of which was draped with black cloth. A hearse glided up from behind, followed by three dark, sleek limousines.

The casket was covered with an enormous American flag. As the police pallbearers carried it on their shoulders up the church steps, the uniformed sergeant barked again:

"*Pree*-sennnnt *Arms!*"

Thousands of white-gloved hands snapped to salute, and a bagpipe began to whine a funeral dirge for a fallen comrade.

He had been a tough, no-nonsense cop, a hero in every sense of the word. Only thirty-five years old when he was killed, but already he had recorded more than three hundred felony arrests and earned twenty-three department citations for bravery. He was the first cop to die in the line of duty in the new year, and he had not died easily. Shot four times by a suspect in an armed robbery. Run over by a car. Then dragged for nearly half a mile until his body was mangled beyond recognition.

And, as always, there was the family. The young widow. A four-year-old son. A nine-month-old daughter.

Seated inside the church, near the family, were the mayor, the police commissioner and other city officials, come to pay their last respects.

The pastor's eulogy was simple, yet eloquent. "His dad's advice was, 'Son, if you want to be successful, choose one God, one woman, one job, and give it all you have.' He chose an honorable profession. He chose to be a policeman in the City of New York, and he gave it all he had. He did not die in vain. He loved being a policeman. He loved the people he served."

A moment of silence. Then, from a rear balcony, the pastor's daughter began to sing a plaintive hymn, "Amazing Grace." A shiver passed through the hundreds of mourners. The widow crumpled forward in her seat. The mayor's shoulders began to quiver. He dropped his face into his hands and unabashedly wept.

When the casket was borne back down the church steps, three police helicopters swooped low in formation, passing directly over the church in a final gesture of tribute. The phalanx of police officers closed ranks once again.

From somewhere unseen a lone bugler began to play taps.

Carolann placed a hand over her heart.

And whether it was the chill air or whether it was something else altogether, many of the cops who had raised a salute with one hand brushed at the corners of their eyes with the other.

It was, after all, so very, very cold.

Some weeks later, a group of one hundred police officers and detectives sat in a barracks-like classroom at the police department's outdoor shooting range. Instead of uniforms, the cops were casually attired in red-and-black checked lumber jackets, down coats, sweatshirts, blue jeans, combat boots or sneakers, and baseball caps. A police instructor with a Fu Manchu mustache stood at the head of the class, one hand holding the stock of a shotgun and the other cradling the barrels.

"This gun is a beast," began the instructor. He eyed the weapon warily, as though it were a coiled rattlesnake that might spring to life in his hands at any moment. "Used correctly, it's formidable. Used incorrectly, it gives us the horrors. If this gun goes off and hits someone in the arm or the leg, forget it, it's gone. It'll take that arm or that leg right off.

"When you load it, keep the barrels tilted slightly down, toward the ground. Once you load the cartridges and snap the action, the safety is on. Make sure the gun is shouldered before the safety is off. There's an awful lot that can go wrong. What do you tell the guy you've been working with for nine years after the gun accidentally goes off and you cut him in half? I'm sorry? I didn't mean for it to happen?"

Some of the cops in the audience squirmed in their seats.

"Now, when you wanna shoot, bring the gun laterally across your body so it doesn't obscure your vision, and you can assume the ready stance. This is no fun gun to shoot. There is considerable recoil. Some people swear this gun kills at *both* ends. As you raise your arm up, you create a little pocket, inside the deltoid muscle. That's where you want that stock."

He turned sideways, showing a profile to his audience, and slowly brought the shotgun up to his shoulder to demonstrate.

"You have to aim this gun with precision. Bring it right up so you can look down the center of the ribs. Lean slightly forward like a boxer. Try to relax . . . aim . . . then fire." The instructor pulled the trigger and it clicked loudly.

"This gun will deliver. If it's gotta be used, it's a very effective anti-personnel weapon. Unfortunately, we sometimes get the headhunter syndrome out here. Some guy who gets his jollies by blowing the head off the target. We try to refrain from doing that. We prefer you to go right for the middle of the target. All the life-support organs are in the center—the heart, the lungs, the spleen, the liver. If this guy is gonna go down, you gotta hit him in the middle. Now, let's go outside and shoot a few rounds."

One by one, the cops marched across the lawn, toward the range. On the way, each was issued a shotgun, plastic goggles to protect the eyes, and a pair of metal headsets to shield the ears against the gun's deafening report.

The first line of shooters, nineteen in all, tacked up their paper targets. Each target displayed the form of a man, crouched, squinting and pointing a revolver. The shooters walked back to the firing line, twenty-five yards away.

The instructor stood behind them. "Load two rounds of rifle shot," he commanded.

"Come to a ready stance . . .

"The line is now ready . . .

"Take up a shoulder position . . .

"Commence firing!"

A wave of sharp booms cracked the air, echoing painfully. Some of the cops who were waiting on the sidelines cupped their ears with their hands.

On the first volley, the shooter who was sixth from the end nicked a shoulder.

On the second volley, the shooter hit a lung.

On the third volley, the shooter took a steadier grip, readjusted the aim, and squeezed the trigger ever so slowly. And then Carolann Natale fired a shotgun blast dead center, right through the heart.

CHAPTER SEVENTEEN

Nothing affected a cop so deeply as the shooting of another cop. In the eyes of the police, it was the most heinous of all crimes, the ultimate affront to the system of law and order that they were all sworn to uphold and defend. An attack on one cop was an attack on all cops. And when it happened, fellow officers reacted swiftly, emotionally, and relentlessly to find the assailant.

One evening, not long after the funeral for the slain officer, Lieutenant Kluge walked briskly into the middle of the task force office, a haggard expression on his face.

"Stand by," he said, waiting for the detectives to stop the chatter and turn in his direction.

"We got a policewoman shot up in Harlem. First one to get shot in the city's history. Two other people shot with her. Let's get some cars up there, on the double."

Within seconds, the entire squad was on its way to the scene.

Carolann rode with Detective Marty Davin and Detective Jim Coffey.

It was dark outside by the time they arrived, and crowds of kids and neighborhood gawkers had gathered across the street from the scene of the shootings, a ground-floor law office on the north side of 126th Street.

Police radio cars had jumped the curb at odd angles and blocked the street to traffic. Their rooftop beacons continued to flash, first red, then white, then red again. Television camera crews, ravenous for footage for the eleven o'clock news, prowled back and forth along the sidewalk, casting blinding beams from portable spotlights across the entrance of the law office.

A detective walked slowly along the street, jotting down the license plate numbers of all the cars parked in the area. Another detective gingerly poked through trash cans, hunting for weapons or other evidence that might have been discarded by the gunmen.

A young black strutted by, making no attempt to conceal his annoyance at the police lines. "I don't give a fuck who got shot," he muttered, just loud enough for the detectives to hear. "For all I know, it could be a sniper. Just let me pass." The detectives ignored him.

An older man wearing a hooded parka and smoking a pipe approached the law office, trying to get a closer look. He was holding an enormous, snarling Great Dane on a leash. "I told him to leave," the man said. "I told him to leave. I told him it was dangerous to stay in this neighborhood." The man apparently was referring to one of the victims, but to Carolann it was not immediately clear which one.

Scores of detectives and uniformed cops began to swarm through the street, questioning bystanders, huddling with commanding officers, heading off on assignments. A temporary command post had been set up in a laundromat several doors down from the law office, and it was packed to the seams with police brass. A faded poster in the front window seemed out of place, heralding an event-gone-by that was totally incongruous with the bloody events of the evening. The poster said: "Welcome John Paul II."

Carolann, Marty Davin, and Jim Coffey affixed their gold

detective shields to their overcoats and headed for the law office. Sergeant Larry Giannetta cut across their path.

"Hey, Sergeant G., what happened?" asked Davin.

Giannetta paused to give them a fast rundown.

"Looks like a ripoff. Two guys come in and ask for the lawyer, Reece, but he's not there. So they leave. Then they come back. One throws a shot at the other lawyer, Jablon. They catch him in the head. The policewoman, Bembry, is just sitting there. She's off duty, came into the law office with her uncle to have their taxes done. The shooter catches her in the side of the face. Shoots the uncle, too. Then they rip a gold chain off the policewoman's neck, take her bag, her gun, her shield. Luckily, she kept her head down after she was hit. Otherwise, they might have finished her off, too."

The victims had already been removed to the hospital, and the police photographers and forensic experts were now going over the office with a fine-tooth comb. Anxious for a look, Carolann stepped through the front door.

It was a cramped and musty two-room office with gray metal filing cabinets piled high along the sides. The walls were covered with faded prints of Japanese girls in kimonos. A Bonsai plant, coated with dust, sat in a corner, looking ridiculously out of place.

In the rear room, where the shootings had occurred, blood was everywhere. Splattered in great gobs across the top of a desk and over a pile of letters and legal documents. Starting to darken and congeal, like drippings from a red wax candle. At the far end of the desk, the telephone receiver was lying off its hook, a small black islet in a puddle of red.

"What's that?" asked Deputy Police Commissioner Ellen Fleysher, pointing to a small white particle on the desk. "A tooth?"

"No, Commissioner," one of the forensic men matter-of-factly answered. "It's brain matter."

On the floor, under the chairs, there was so much blood that it looked like a small lake had formed. Lying upside-down in the center of the lake were a pair of black-framed eyeglasses. The glasses had literally been blown off the head of one of the victims.

Marty Davin stepped outside and moved off to canvass the neighborhood for possible witnesses. He was particularly intrigued by a grundgy-looking record shop, several doors down. Stenciled on the window were the words "Records, Tapes, Bambu, Incense, Goodies, Accessories," an inventory that seemed suspiciously open to interpretation. The shop looked closed, but Davin, joined by Carolann and two other detectives, rapped at the door anyway. Then he rang the buzzer.

"Who is it?" shouted a voice, somewhere inside.

"Police," answered Davin. "Open the door, we wanna talk to you for a second."

"You sure you is police officers?"

"Yeah, yeah, come on, open the door, we just wanna talk."

After several more minutes of haggling, the door buzzed open and the detectives walked inside. For a few moments, they found themselves in total darkness. Suddenly the room was bathed in flickering pink fluorescent light and the store took on the psychedelic ambiance of a discotheque. Incense, pungent and cloying, saturated the air. Rock music blared from concealed speakers. When the detectives' eyes adjusted to the bright light, they noticed a pane of bullet-proof glass on top of the counter, running the entire length of the store. Behind the glass stood a young man, eyeing them nervously.

"Lemme see some I.D.," he said.

Davin flashed his shield.

The man unlocked a small gate, permitting the detectives to crawl under the bullet-proof glass, behind the counter and down toward the rear of the shop.

"We're detectives and we're investigating that incident down the street," Davin told the young man, who was standing now between a television set and two stereo speakers, all turned up to maximum volume. "Whaddya hear? Whaddya see?"

"I ain't heard nothin' and I ain't seen nothin'," the young man replied, volunteering his answer just a little too quickly.

With a sixth sense, Davin eyed the counter and spotted two stacks of money, neatly piled. Nearby lay a couple of loose joints. Davin smiled to himself. "Better not leave your money lying out there like that," he advised. The young man began to fidget.

"Hey, we're not lookin' to bust you," Davin reassured him. "We're just lookin' to find out what happened down the block. Would you help us if you had heard anything? Would you give us a call?"

"Yessir, yessir," replied the young man, now a paragon of compliance.

"But will you cooperate?"

"Yessir, yessir, any way we can, we'll cooperate. We don't want no law comin' down on us."

Outside, one of the other detectives, who was black, told Davin: "Drugs, man, drugs. They not worried about the police. They worried about some guy comin' in and rippin' 'em off."

Wise to the tricks of the trade, the detective began to cackle like a hen.

By the time Carolann arrived at St. Luke's Hospital, the main lobby was jammed with people. Cops were milling about, waiting for some word on the condition of their wounded friend and colleague, Police Officer Mary Bembry. All the brass were there. The mayor, too. Newspaper and television reporters waited impatiently outside the front door, hungering for more details and fretting over deadlines. It was, after all, a major story. A thirty-two-year-old policewoman, the mother of two teenage boys, shot in the face and seriously wounded along with two other victims. Officer Bembry had been the first woman cop to be shot since the New York City Police Department began hiring women in the late 1890s.

A press conference was hastily arranged. Flushed with anger, the mayor declared: "We've got to rout these animals out. They shot them down and then ripped a necklace off her throat. These aren't people. These are animals. It's an outrage that they are on the streets."

As the mayor spoke, Carolann skirted the mob of cops and reporters and darted around the back way to the emergency room. There, she spotted a familiar face, Detective Dottie Johnson. Twelve years earlier, Dottie and Carolann had been among the same group of ten women to make the cutoff and be appointed to the force; Dottie was number nine, Carolann number ten. Dottie had since earned her gold detective shield, worked undercover in narcotics, and advanced to detective second grade. Now she was assigned to the Twenty-sixth Precinct Detective Unit.

"Dottie!" shouted Carolann.

"Oh, Carol, hi!"

"Who's got the case?"

Dottie rolled her eyes back into her head, "I do."

"Oh, good," said Carolann. "Listen, let me give you a hand. I'm with the task force now. They sent me over to help out. Did you get a chance to talk to Mary?"

"I talked to her for a few minutes," said Dottie. "But I couldn't get too much. Just the basic story. She's in no shape to go into details."

"How about the other two?"

"Well, the uncle is being operated on right this minute. The attorney is in intensive care. He's on the machine."

"Did you see him?"

"No. Why don't you come with me and we'll see if we can talk to him?"

The two women flashed their gold shields and a guard waved them through a door, into the intensive care section.

Propped up on a hospital bed, the attorney lay unconscious and motionless, barely breathing. His complexion was ghostly white. IVs had been jabbed into the veins of his arms and a tube inserted up his nose. Other tubes ran from his arms and legs to a life-support machine, and an electric monitor kept pace with the feeble beat of his heart. His head was swathed with bandages, now soaked with blood.

"Any hope?" asked Dottie.

The nurse standing by the bed simply shook her head.

Dottie headed back to the Twenty-sixth Precinct to brief her superiors. Carolann returned to the emergency room, in search of the wounded policewoman. Perhaps she might still be able to provide a description of the gunmen before she was wheeled into the operating room.

The bullet had slammed into the right side of Mary Bembry's face, shattered her jaw, knocked out two teeth, and lodged under her tongue. Her cheek was swollen and discolored when they wheeled her out and she was spitting up mouthfuls of blood. When the attendants pushed her onto a waiting elevator, Carolann stepped inside with them.

"Mary, I'm Detective Natale from the task force. I'm gonna stay with you."

Woozy from painkillers and sedatives, Mary blinked her eyes and managed a faint nod, but was unable to talk. The elevator arrived at an upper floor, where the surgeons were waiting. Just as the attendants were about to wheel Mary off, Carolann touched her lightly on the arm.

"Don't worry, Mary, you're gonna be fine."

And then she was gone, down the hall, into the operating room and out of sight.

At the far end of the hall, Detectives Jerry Manero and Marty Martinez were crisscrossing the floor, peeking into one room after another, trying to find Mary's wounded uncle.

"Hey, you know where this fellow is?" Manero asked a nurse. The nurse shrugged, then continued on her way.

Irritated, Manero whispered to Martinez, "Lucky they know they got someone here who's been shot."

A surgeon passed by. Manero grabbed him by the arm. "Hey, doc, any chance of talking to the uncle before you do the operation?"

The surgeon, who looked like an alien from outer space in his green jumpsuit, green cap and green slippers, shook his head. "He's got two tubes in his side and one in his throat. He can't talk to you now." The surgeon walked back into the operating room.

Manero and Martinez spotted Carolann at the far end of the hall, and the three regrouped for that one activity in which detectives seemed to specialize: waiting.

Fifteen minutes later, another surgeon walked out of the operating room. His white smock was splattered with blood-stains. "Are you police officers?" he asked.

The three detectives looked up.

"We can give you a bullet. The uncle just died."

Manero started towards the operating room, but a nurse intercepted him. "Sorry, but you can't go in like that. You'll have to put on a sanitary gown."

With the help of two nurses, Manero struggled to squeeze

into a jumpsuit, but he was only partially successful. Since the jumpsuit was about three sizes too small, the detective was forced to leave the midsection unbuttoned. Undeterred, he trotted off toward the operating room, holding his hands up in the air like a surgeon on his way to scrub up.

When he returned, he was holding a plastic cup containing a small, gold-colored bullet, still flecked with blood.

Carolann couldn't resist.

"Jerry, you really look cute in that outfit."

"Congratulations, Carol," Jerry shot back, his voice muffled by a surgical mask. "It's twins. And you're going to be just fine."

"Really cute, Jerry."

"Quiet, Carol," said Jerry, who was now engaged in hand-to-hand combat with his jumpsuit, which refused to peel off easily.

Several other surgeons had joined the detectives in examining the bullet. One took the plastic cup from Manero and held it up to the light.

"Is that a .38?" asked Carolann.

"Looks like a .45 to me," said Jerry.

"Looks like a .38 to me," said the surgeon.

"Just don't rub the bullet," Marty Martinez warned. "We need it for evidence."

One of the doctors attempted to explain the cause of death. Tracing a forefinger across Manero's chest to illustrate, he said: "The bullet entered the left side, traversed the liver, then hit the spleen."

The latest word on the third victim, the lawyer, was that he was paralyzed from the neck down and probably would die. Of the three, only the policewoman was likely to survive.

Carolann shook her head. "If Mary hadn't put her head down and pretended to be dead . . ."

But there was no need to complete the sentence. Everyone knew exactly what she was thinking.

When the detectives returned downstairs to the emergency room, the wife and children of the dead uncle were just being ushered into a private office. They did not yet know that he had expired on the operating table. A hospital administrator was waiting for the surgeon to come down and tell them.

In an adjoining office, Carolann, Jerry Manero, and Marty Martinez began to interview a hospital employee who had received an anonymous telephone tip about the shootings. A female caller, possibly a crank, had phoned the hospital switchboard to say that the gunman was hiding out at a West Side address. The detectives were pressing for more details when, suddenly, from the hall outside, came a horrible piercing wail.

"Oh God, no-no-no-please-no-Daddy-*nooooooo!*"

Carolann yanked open the door just as a young girl, the slain uncle's daughter, collapsed in the arms of a nurse. A boy was slumped against the wall, beside himself with grief. Dazed by it all, he whimpered over and over again, "Mommy, Mommy, Mommy . . ." Then he became hysterical and hurled himself to the floor. The surgeon had finally broken the grim news.

An older brother pulled the boy to his feet. Two sisters were quickly at his side. Gripping all three firmly by the shoulders, the older brother drew their heads close to his own and the four children melded together in grief, like statues in a marble sculpture.

"He didn't suffer," murmured their mother, struggling bravely to maintain her own composure. "He didn't suffer."

It was close to midnight when the detectives assigned to the case assembled in a large room on the second floor of the Twenty-sixth Precinct stationhouse for an update on the shootings. Like college students attending a lecture, they sat in small chairs with writing boards attached, scribbling notes and smoking cigarettes. There were nearly thirty detectives in the room and Carolann, pen and notepad in hand, was among them.

Richard Nicastro, chief of all the Manhattan detectives, sat at a table, peering impatiently over the tops of his bifocals. Lieutenant Kluge, nattily dressed in a dark-gray suit with white pinstripes, stood in front of a blackboard. Holding a piece of chalk in one hand, he looked like an orchestra conductor about to begin the opening movement of a symphony.

Nicastro kicked things off. "All right, one guy at a time. Let's take it from the top. You got one dead, the other guy's on the machine. We may wind up with two dead."

Kluge took over. "What we wanna do is put the whole puzzle together so we have a little direction. What we're interested in now is a description of the shooter."

For the next hour, the detectives batted the case back and forth, rehashing the sequence of events, adding some new details, disputing others, mulling descriptions given by eyewitnesses, sifting out false leads, firming up real ones, trying to figure out exactly "what went down."

Dottie Johnson, the only detective to get an interview with the wounded policewoman before she underwent surgery, gave this account:

"The shooter goes out, then he comes back in again. He first fires on the lawyer, second on Mary, third on the uncle. He was a male black, about eighteen, wearing a blue snorkel jacket. When the lawyer gets hit, Mary turns and gets fired on. She figured he's gonna shoot her again, so she remains very still and pretends to be dead. He grabs the chain off her neck, then he grabs the bag. He opens the bag, sees the gun and shield, then he says, 'Oh shit, I shot a cop!'"

Sergeant Pat Breen advanced to the blackboard and began sketching the floor plan of the law office.

"Let's get to the most important part," said Lieutenant Kluge, attempting to steer the discussion back on the main track. "Solvability. Anybody got any witnesses who they could put at the scene? If so, that could be the ball game."

Stepping up to the blackboard, Kluge began making notations on the floor plan already drafted by Breen. Bit by bit, like an artist creating a landscape, he sketched in the locations of witnesses, times, directions, entry routes, escape routes. Within a few minutes, the floor plan was obliterated by numbers, arrows, circles, and dotted lines. It began to resemble the obscure jottings of a physicist.

Nicastro was growing restless. "Now let's see what we can do to scoop these guys up."

In the early morning hours that followed, there were two developments that gave an even greater impetus to the investigation. First, just hours after Officer Bembry was gunned down, a second officer, a decoy cop, was shot to death while chasing a suspected drug dealer down an alley in another part of Harlem. And later in the morning, the lawyer who was wounded with Officer Bembry and her uncle succumbed to his wounds.

He died at the hospital just before dawn.

Over the next few days, Carolann played a utility role, assisting the detectives from the Twenty-sixth Precinct who had primary responsibility for investigating the shootings. Arriving at the stationhouse by 8 a.m. each day, she would begin by reading the other detectives' reports, or "fives" as they were known. Then she would cull through mug shots of possible suspects, talk by telephone with relatives of the victims and review court cases of defendants who had demonstrated a similar modus operandi during the commission of an armed robbery. Lieutenant Bob Gibbons of the task force had taken charge of the investigation, and periodically the detectives would gather around a desk in his office to sip coffee and verbally replay the entire crime from scratch.

"I know those little sons-of-bitches are somewhere between here and 115th Street," one detective said one morning. "They're punks, nothing but punks. They just walk in and start firing. Seventeen- and eighteen-year-old kids. They got scared, so they started shooting."

Each afternoon, Carolann would accompany either Dottie Johnson or one of the other detectives to St. Luke's Hospital for followup interviews with Officer Bembry. The wounded policewoman had been moved to a private room after her surgery and was under round-the-clock guard. Day and night, a policeman was posted outside her door.

On the first day after the shootings, Mary Bembry was groggy and still spitting up blood.

On the second day, she seemed a bit stronger. Because of her wound, her speech was a bit garbled. She was able to give the detectives another account of her ordeal, but it was still sketchy. They needed more details.

So, on the third day, the detectives brought in the hypnotist. Carolann made the introduction. "Mary, this is Sergeant Darnell." Despite the large piece of gauze taped to her swollen right cheekbone, Police Officer Mary Bembry managed a smile.

Sgt. James Darnell looked like anything but a cop. He wore

a smartly tailored dark suit and a pale blue shirt. His neatly combed gray hair, brush-like mustache, and finely chiseled features gave him the well-heeled mien of a man of breeding and wealth. His manner was somber. His humor was bone dry. And his gaze was eerily and irresistibly riveting.

Taking a seat by Mary's bed, Darnell began, "Now, Mary, I would like you to look up as far as you can see, as though you were trying to look through a hole in the top of your head." His voice was as smooth and as sweet as hot molasses. "Yes, that's it . . . very good."

"While you are looking up, Mary, slowly close your eyelids . . . take a deep breath . . . exhale . . . let your eyes relax and your body float."

Mary Bembry's head eased back into her pillow and the tension seemed to drain from her body, as if each of her joints had been loosened a notch by an invisible wrench.

Darnell continued, his voice undulating gently, slowly drawing her deeper and deeper into a trance. "As you concentrate on your body floating, you allow one hand to rise up in the air like a toy balloon . . . good, good . . . as your hand floats higher and higher, you go deeper and deeper into relaxation. You are becoming more tranquil, more calm, more relaxed with every breath you take."

Darnell's voice became even smoother and softer, seductively mesmerizing. So much so that Carolann and the other detectives in the room had to pinch themselves periodically to keep from falling under his spell.

"Now, as I count back from ten to zero, you will relax even more deeply. When I reach the count of zero, you will be very relaxed, in a deep hypnotic state, and ready to follow my instructions. "Ten . . . nine . . . eight . . . seven . . . six . . . five . . . four . . . three . . . two . . . one . . . zero.

"Now, Mary, you will be able to remain in this deeply relaxed state. Nothing will disturb you. I'd like you to let your mind float back in time and space, back to the evening of February eleventh, and you see yourself at the corner of 126th Street and Amsterdam Avenue. You are walking along with your uncle.

"Now, tell me what happened next."

* * *

When it was over, Darnell concluded that the decision to hypnotize Mary had been a mistake. She had been able to re-create that awful moment when the gunmen burst into the law office and started shooting, but her recollections were so vivid that she was swept up by a powerful release of emotion and fear, and she wept hysterically. Whatever new details were gleaned from the hypnotic session were simply not crucial enough to justify the trauma. It was just too painful. And too soon.

Disheartened, but still determined, the detectives busied themselves with other tasks.

During the next week, Carolann helped voucher the bloody clothing of the dead men for safekeeping, in case it was needed later as evidence. Then she arranged for the police department to release $125 in cash, found in the trousers of the slain uncle, to his widow. Later, she drove to the Westchester mansion of the murdered lawyer to interview his widow, trying to learn about credit cards and other valuables that might have been plucked from his body after he was gunned down.

The case was now into its second week, and the widow was beginning to have doubts. The killers might never be found. But Carolann reassured her.

"Don't worry, there's no doubt we'll get the people responsible for your husband's murder. No doubt whatsoever."

A bitter cold night in February, eleven days after the shootings. The streets of Manhattan's Upper West Side were dark and deserted, eerily quiet. It was 3 a.m.

Out on routine patrol, Detective Mike Sheehan and Police Officer Steve Davis turned their radio car into 107th Street, heading toward Columbus Avenue. Deliberately, they drove the wrong way up 107th and kept the headlights off. This was one of the simple ploys that the cops often used to gain an extra element of surprise when scanning the tenements and side streets for drug dealers, gunmen, and other mischief makers. Just a week earlier, they had scooped up a kid with a gun and a quarter-ounce of cocaine, all because he looked the wrong way for an oncoming patrol car before attempting his getaway.

At Columbus Avenue, Davis turned the car north, again bucking the flow of traffic. As the car neared 108th Street, a young black man poked his head out of a doorway, looking as cautious as a groundhog. Unaware of the patrol car inching up from the south, he glanced only to the north. Then, satisfied that the coast was clear, he turned and motioned toward the hallway. A second youth stepped outside behind him.

Something not kosher here, Sheehan thought. "Hey, Stevie," he whispered to his partner. "What the hell's this guy up to? That building's all Dominicans, isn't it. What's a black guy doin' comin' outta there?"

Officer Davis studied the building for a moment. "Mikey, you made a gun collar there last year, remember?"

"What say we check it out?" said Sheehan.

As the patrol car came closer, the two youths spun around and spotted it. Glancing back over their shoulders, they began walking down 108th Street, whispering nervously to each other, quickening the pace. Ten feet behind, the two cops slowly followed.

The two youths split up, one walking straight ahead, the other crossing the street.

Sheehan unholstered his gun. "Where you wanna take 'em, Stevie?"

"Let's wait till they reach the avenue," said Davis.

Suddenly, one of the youths came to a halt. Davis slammed the brake pedal to the floor. Rolling down his window, Sheehan yelled to the other youth: "Hey, fellah, c'mere! Like to see you for a second."

Just as the youth neared Sheehan's door, Davis sounded an alarm. "Mikey, I can't see that other fuck!" Shoving open the front door, he vaulted out of the driver's seat.

The second youth was standing there, just behind the radio car, and he was trying to pull something from his shirt. Davis took three giant steps and dropped him with a flying tackle.

"Mikey!" he shouted back to the car. "This fuck has a gun!"

Sheehan's fingers tightened around the revolver he was holding in his lap. The youth standing near his door began to ease one hand into a jacket pocket.

But Sheehan had his gun out the window and pointed at his head before he could withdraw his hand. "Take your hands outta your pockets," he calmly ordered, "or I'll blow your fucking head off."

In a flash, the youth was off and running, sprinting toward Manhattan Avenue.

"Stevie!" shouted Sheehan. "You all right?"

"Yeah, I'm okay, but get that other guy. He's carrying a piece!"

Sliding over to the driver's seat, Sheehan plucked the receiver off the radio and urgently called for back-up units. "Twenty-Four Edward in pursuit, north on Manhattan Avenue and One-Oh-Eight Street!" he shouted. "Ten-Eighty-Five, forthwith!"

Screeching up Manhattan Avenue, Sheehan caught up with the second youth just as he turned west on 109th Street. When the youth paused in front of the building on the corner, 20 West 109th Street, an ironic recollection flashed through Mike Sheehan's mind. Four decades earlier, that was the very same building in which Sheehan's father had lived after coming to this country from Ireland.

The youth was heading east now, toward Central Park West. Suddenly, he lost his footing and tumbled to the pavement. At almost the same instant, the speeding radio car hit a patch of ice in the road and skidded right past him into the intersection. Sheehan was out of the car in a second, his revolver drawn.

In a panic now, the youth tossed his own gun into the snow and tried to make one last run for it. But Sheehan broad-jumped a mound of snow, grabbed hold of his shoulders, and slammed him roughly into the side of a building.

"Fuck you, man!" gasped the punk. "I didn't do nothin'!"

He struggled furiously to shake off his captor. But when he felt the cold, hard barrel of a .38 revolver planted snugly behind his ear, his body went limp.

"All right you motherfucker," warned Sheehan. "Just get your hands up in the air. Now!"

"What's your name?" asked Sheehan, clicking a pair of handcuffs on the young man's wrists. He looked to be about nineteen or twenty years old.

"Michael," he whispered, his voice nearly inaudible.

"Michael what?" the cop spat back.

"McAvoy."

"Whaddya got in your pockets?"

"Nothin'." His throat was so dry now and his tongue so swollen that he could barely mouth answers to the cop's questions. Sheehan had seen it all before; the classic symptoms of the nervous liar.

Reaching inside McAvoy's trouser pockets, Sheehan pulled out a wet and sticky clump of rolled-up paper. He held it up to his flashlight and discovered it was a wad of money, soaked with blood. McAvoy's pants leg was bloodied, too, yet he did not appear to be injured. Sheehan read him his rights. Just then, two squad cars pulled up and more officers jumped out to assist.

When McAvoy and the other young man were marched back into the building on 108th Street where they first were spotted, it was only a matter of time before the posse of cops found their victim. A Hispanic man, lying on the floor of one of the apartments, had apparently been shot to death by the two youths during a stickup.

But when the officers took McAvoy's gun—the .38-caliber snub-nosed special he had tossed into the snow bank—down to the police department's Ballistics Unit, they made an even more startling discovery.

It was the same weapon that had wounded Policewoman Mary Bembry and killed the two men with her.

After undergoing hours of grilling by detectives at the Twenty-fourth Precinct stationhouse, the two young suspects implicated themselves not only in the shooting of the policewoman and the murder of the Hispanic man on 108th Street, but in dozens of other shootings and robberies as well. They even gave detectives the name of an accomplice, who was quickly arrested outside his home in the Bronx and brought back to the stationhouse for questioning.

When all was said and done, the trio of stickup men admitted to more than a dozen murders. They were clearly one of the most cold-blooded gangs in the city's history.

Euphoric over their capture, the police department and the district attorneys from Manhattan and the Bronx called a press conference to announce the good news. Television cameras rolled, flashbulbs popped and reporters scribbled away furiously as Detective Sheehan, Officer Davis, and many of the detectives from the Twenty-fourth Precinct, the Twenty-sixth Precinct, and the task force basked deservedly in the limelight.

The only one missing was Carolann Natale.

As luck would have it, it was her day off.

CHAPTER EIGHTEEN

There were some cases—like the shooting of the police-woman and the slaying of the two men with her—that ended on a triumphant note. With the suspects in custody, confessions on tape, and the murder weapon in hand, all the pieces fell neatly into place. What's more, the chances for court convictions were excellent. For weeks after the arrests the detectives would discuss the investigation with great animation, taking stock of its many twists and turns and rehashing the highlights, like Monday morning quarterbacks savoring Sunday's big victory.

But there were other cases that ended on a note of a different sort.

One morning, as Carolann and Dominick Bologna returned to the task force office from Upper Manhattan, where they had been investigating the kidnaping of a newborn baby, they were greeted by Sergeant Larry Giannetta. His expression was unsmiling and grim.

"C'mon, let's go," Giannetta said. "We got a double in an apartment down by Washington Square. Father and kid, blown away with a shotgun."

On the way, inside the car, Carolann and Dominick began to brace themselves psychologically. Dominick had seen shotgun victims before, but never children. Anticipating that the scene would be grisly and anxious to spare Carolann the trauma of witnessing it, he tried to dissuade her in advance from entering the room where the bodies had been found.

"Jeez," he began, "I don't like to see things like that. You don't have to go in, Carol. There's no need for both of us to go in."

But Carolann, who was always sensitive about receiving special treatment that might be given because she was a woman, balked at the suggestion. "Why should you go and I not go?" she asked.

"Well," reasoned Dominick, "I'm volunteering to go in. It doesn't make sense for both of us to be going."

"Look, Dominick," countered Carolann, "we both have human feelings. What makes you think you can accept this any better because you're a male and I'm a female?"

Dominick held firm. "I can't see any points being made whether you go in or you don't go in because of the fact that you're a female, Carol. I know plenty of male detectives who won't go in a room with dead bodies."

They argued back and forth a few minutes more, but in the end Dominick prevailed. It was agreed. He would go alone into the room with the bodies. Carolann would remain outside, unless it was absolutely necessary for her to assist.

The building was one of those grand old pre-war high rises with a canopied entrance, fronting Washington Square Park. A forensic truck and a couple of squad cars already were parked outside. Television camera crews, drawn like bees to honey, were swarming around the entrance, trying to question police officers who came or went, confronting startled tenants, buttonholing anyone and everyone who might be able to give them any information about the victims.

Off to one side, a detective sergeant from the local precinct stood quietly, jotting some notes in a pad. He was quick to give Carolann and Dominick an update on the case. It wasn't a double homicide after all, but a homicide and a suicide. The father, a successful attorney, had shot his eight-year-old son in the head, then turned the shotgun on himself. A suicide note had been found inside the apartment. Also found was a receipt for the shotgun, purchased just a day earlier from a gun shop in New Jersey. The mother, also an attorney, was out of the city on business, attending a legal convention on the West Coast. The police were still attempting to locate her to break the tragic news.

"Terrible, just terrible," murmured the elderly elevator operator as he took the two task force detectives up to the tenth floor.

Just outside the elevator bank, tacked to a wall, was a cardboard sign that warned: "Crime Scene. Do Not Pass. New York City Police Department." At the far end of the carpeted hall, a policeman and a policewoman had been posted as sentries. Carolann and Dominick flashed their badges, then stepped around them into the apartment.

Once inside, they stopped to get their bearings. It was an enormous apartment, lavishly furnished and with a spectacular view of the park. They were standing in the main foyer. From the first bedroom, just off to the right, came muted voices. Other detectives, discussing the case. Dominick stepped inside to let them know that the back-up team had arrived. Carolann routinely followed.

And then, before she could check herself and backtrack, she saw it. Just a blur, glimpsed only for a few seconds, but it was a sight she would never forget: the man and boy sprawled lifelessly across the bed, the blood-soaked blanket and pillows, the shotgun resting across the father's torso, the clots of blood and tissue splattered across the floors and walls, the bone fragments on the carpet, propelled by the force of the blasts clear across the room.

Dominick whirled in his tracks, dismayed that Carolann had wandered onto the very scene from which he had been determined to shield her.

"No, Carol," he said firmly. Holding one hand in front of

her face, he used the other to gently steer her back out the door. "There's no need for you to see this."

Numbly, unable to make her brain accept what her eyes had just seen, Carolann retreated. She drifted further down the hall, toward a second door, and stepped inside. Now she was standing in a child's room, done up brightly in oranges, greens and yellows. In the middle of the room was a bunk bed, covered with large fluffy pillows. On the shelves were children's things, toys, books, a football, a record player. A painted rocking horse sat in a corner. On the floor near the bed, there were small shoes, more toys, some stuffed animals, a couple of pillows.

For a few moments, she stared blankly at the pillows, not quite able to make sense of things, baffled by the bloodstains on them. Then, like a jolt, it hit her. The little boy had been shot here, probably while sleeping on the pillows, then moved to the other bedroom.

The shock was wearing off, reality was beginning to sink in. This was all real, all happening. Not a television show or a movie. Not some kind of trick done with props and makeup. Carolann glanced around again at the child's room, so warm and cheerful. For a moment, she was afraid she might cry.

In the hall outside, a uniformed police officer staggered by, pasty-faced and wobbly. He had just come from the main bedroom, where the bodies were. He was respirating rapidly, taking great gulps of air, deliberately exaggerating the pace of his breathing to increase the oxygen intake and stave off the nausea. When he saw Carolann, he rolled his eyes back into his head. There was no need to speak. His facial gesture said it all.

Another man passed by, one of the detectives. "No matter how many times you see it, you never get used to it," he muttered softly.

Back in the living room, more composed now, Carolann began to interview the housekeeper who had found the bodies. She was a West Indian woman, in her fifties, and there was a sing-song lilt to her speech, a remnant of her native patois. As was her practice, she had let herself into the apartment that morning with a key. She had worked for nearly a half hour before stumbling upon the bodies.

They spoke briefly about the dead man, his total devotion

to his wife and son, his periodic bouts of depression, his visits to a psychiatrist.

"Tell me," said Carolann, "do you remember ever seeing him laugh?"

It seemed an odd question, and for a few moments the housekeeper merely stared at Carolann, not quite believing she had asked it. But then, when the significance of the question began to register, the woman replied: "You know, I don't think I ever really did. He never laughed."

As the housekeeper spoke, Carolann's gaze drifted past her shoulder, to the wall just behind. Hanging there were enlarged photos of the family—the little boy, swinging happily in the park; the father and mother holding hands, all three riding together in a horse-drawn buggy, the little boy building sand castles at the beach. A beautiful family, loving and loved. The wall of photos looked like a shrine.

From somewhere in the living room came an odd, whirring noise. Carolann turned and noticed a cage on the floor in a far corner, just below the window. Inside the cage were two gerbils, furry, mouselike creatures, pawing furiously at a plastic wheel and making it spin. The gerbils had been the little boy's pets.

Dominick had finished in the master bedroom. While the other detectives waited for the medical examiner to complete her inspection of the bodies, he and Carolann decided to canvass the rest of the building, hoping to find a neighbor who might offer an explanation for the tragic deaths and pinpoint the time of occurrence.

At the far end of the hall, a man of about sixty was home.

"Sorry to disturb you," Dominick told the man, who had opened his door just a fraction and was peering out cautiously at the two visitors. "We're detectives and there's been an incident down the hall, in apartment 10-F. We were wondering if you might have heard anything."

"Ten-F?" repeated the man. "Those are my neighbors. Anything wrong?"

Carolann answered. "There's been a shooting."

"A shooting?" gasped the man, clearly stunned. "Nobody got hurt, did they?"

"I'm sorry to say that Mr. Kinsman is dead," said Carolann.

The man went ashen. "Oh, my God, no," he moaned. "Such a lovely man, it can't be true. Such a wonderful father..." Then, a horrible afterthought crossed his mind. "But what about the little boy?"

Carolann gave him the rest of it. "The little boy is dead, too."

The man staggered backwards, as if reeling from a punch. "Oh, my God, no, no," he moaned over and over again. He looked like he was about to collapse, and Dominick was quickly at his side, guiding him toward a chair.

"Mr. Corwin, why don't we just sit down a moment and talk. We're concerned about your health and we don't want you to get sick. There's been enough tragedy today."

They stayed with him only briefly. Other than confirming the housekeeper's story—that the dead man had been a loving husband and devoted father—there was little more that Mr. Corwin could add.

As they were leaving, another neighbor, a young woman, got off the elevator. "Who are *you?*" she snapped when Dominick approached her in the hallway. Shaken by the news about her neighbors and already accosted in the lobby by some of the reporters, the woman's nerves were raw.

Her manner softened measurably when Dominick and Carolann identified themselves. She even invited them inside her apartment. Dominick helped her carry her shopping bags. But then, just as the detectives started to question her, the telephone rang.

"Yes, yes, I know," they could hear the woman saying. "The police are here talking to me, right now...Yes, I know...No, I won't tell them anything...I'm not stupid..."

The woman hung up. "That was my husband. He's an attorney. He says I shouldn't tell you anything."

Carolann began to bristle. "Yeah, we're very familiar with attorneys and just that sort of advice," she remarked sarcastically. Then, trying to reason with the woman: "I hope you are aware, Madam, that anything we discuss here—it's not our policy to give it to the press. Anything you tell us will be held in strict confidence."

But the woman merely shrugged. She had decided to follow her husband's advice.

"Don't let it bother you, Carol," murmured Dominick on the way out of the apartment. "People are strange. Their priorities are strange."

Some of the other neighbors were more cooperative.

One told of hearing strange sounds—popping or pinging noises—sometime after midnight the night before. They might have been gunshots; he couldn't be certain. Having never heard gunshots before, he wasn't sure what they sounded like.

Another neighbor said that only the morning before he had encountered Mr. Kinsman on a street corner and asked him if he might like to share a taxicab. "No," the man had replied, "I have a doctor's appointment." But if he did indeed have a doctor's appointment, the detectives later learned, he never showed up to keep it.

And a third neighbor told of seeing the man and his little boy the previous afternoon, out on the sidewalk just around the corner from the building. The two were sitting together happily at a makeshift stand, father and son, selling popcorn and lemonade.

On the way back uptown, Carolann and Dominick said little to each other about the double slaying. Lost in their own thoughts, they barely spoke at all.

Then, at one point, Carolann asked: "You all right?"

"Fine," answered Dominick, but he did not seem anxious to continue the conversation.

"I would have liked to talk to that man's psychiatrist," said Carolann.

"Why?" wondered Dominick. "What would you have hoped to gain from the knowledge?"

"For myself. To understand what I've just seen . . . and can't accept. Maybe if I talked to the psychiatrist, it would help me to understand."

"But it still wouldn't change what happened," said Dominick. "You can't dwell on these things."

There was a pause. Then Carolann said, "You're right." And that was the last time that either detective would mention the case.

That night, Carolann returned home from work about 8 p.m. She tried to pass the evening by watching television. But none of the programs interested her, so she switched the set off. For a while, she glanced at a book, a Gothic mystery. But she found herself unable to concentrate and soon tossed it aside. Finally, she took a hot shower, turned off the lights, and went to bed.

But not once during that interminable night was she able to fall asleep.

CHAPTER NINETEEN

By the following week, things had more or less returned to normal in the task force. The detectives were preoccupied with a batch of new murder cases. The tragic homicide-suicide that had taken the lives of the father and his young son was all but forgotten. Sitting around the office on a Saturday morning, Carolann sipped slowly from her mug of coffee as she listened to Dominick Bologna describe the latest misfortune to befall his car.

"I'm sittin' up in Harlem one day, waitin' for another detective to meet me for a stakeout," Dominick was saying. He unwrapped the cellophane from a fresh cigar as he spoke. "I'm lookin' at a newspaper, just mindin' my own business, when suddenly, out of the corner of my eye, I see this old Puerto Rican guy comin' down the street. He's pushin' a box spring mattress in front of him, on those little wheels. Must have found it in the garbage or something. Only he's havin' trouble keepin' the damn thing under control. Keeps swayin' from side to side. And I'm sayin' to myself, 'Oh boy, here it comes.' Sure enough, he gets up to my car and—Bang!—he plows right into the side with the mattress. Leaves a big scratch in the paint."

Dominick turned toward the other detectives, a pained expression on his face. "Now I ask you, what the hell's this guy doin' walking down the sidewalk with a mattress?"

"Probably a psychiatrist makin' a house call," suggested Carl Sgrizzi. Judging by the nods of approval from the rest of the squad, it was an assessment that showed commendable insight.

"Hey, look at this!" shouted one of the other detectives, pointing to a bulletin that had been tacked to the wall, right below a cluster of old Wanted posters.

Some of the men began reading over his shoulder. The bulletin was a communique from the police department's Inspections Division, alerting all officers and detectives who had been on active duty with the Armed Forces or in the active reserve that they could now take certain holidays off with pay. Among the holidays: Veterans Day, Memorial Day, and the Fourth of July.

While the other detectives eagerly studied the communique, trying to figure out exactly how much time they had coming, Carolann sat by herself at her desk, forlorn and pouting. Finally, she blurted out: "Well, I don't think that's fair. I can't get any time off for military service. I should get two holidays just for giving birth to two children."

"Okay, Carol," shot back Detective Bob Catalano. "We'll give you Labor Day." And the rest of the detectives promptly broke into laughter.

Just then, the telephone rang.

It was one of the task force sergeants, calling from the field to ask that Carolann, Dominick, and Carl shoot up to the Twenty-fifth Precinct in Harlem to help out on a kidnaping case.

The superintendent of a building had disappeared, and the detectives from the local precinct were convinced that he had been abducted by some of his own tenants, maybe even murdered. In recent months, the super had been burglarizing their apartments, stealing their furniture, their clothes, their spare cash, even the beds of their children. For this thief, nothing was sacred.

Robbed of her groceries, one eighty-two-year-old lady was so angered by the super's thievery that she mixed up a caustic solution in a saucer, knocked at the super's door and, when the door opened, heaved the solution in the door opener's face.

Only to discover that it was not the super who had opened the door, but the super's wife.

The wife was not seriously hurt. But the eighty-two-year-old lady was arrested by the police on a charge of attempted murder. And, to add insult to injury, while she was at the precinct being booked, the super returned home, broke into her apartment again, and stripped it clean of every last piece of furniture and clothing she owned.

For the other neighbors, that was the last straw. Banding together vigilante style, four of them had marched into the local bar, dragged the super from his stool and beaten him bloody and senseless. Then they tossed him in the back of a waiting car and drove off. The thinking was that they probably had dumped him in the river.

For the task force detectives, the assignment was a routine one. Canvass the super's building. Talk to the tenants. Get descriptions of the victim and the suspects. Find out when they were last seen, what they were wearing, who they spoke to, etc.

The building was a cocoa-colored tenement, a hedgerow of garbage cans its only landscaping. On either side there were more tenements, their once neat facades now marred by obscene graffiti or billboards in Spanish or stenciled signs that cautioned "No Loitering," "No Ball Playing" and "Post No Bills." Young men, their eyes red and puffy from too much cheap booze, loitered on stoops or in doorways. Old men hobbled by slowly on canes. In the street, two small boys kicked a red ball back and forth, chattering with delight, oblivious to their dismal surroundings.

The inside of the tenement was even more depressing than the outside. The halls were dark, narrow and tunnel-like, their pockmarked green walls illuminated at intervals by bare fifty-watt lightbulbs in the ceiling. Many of the apartment doors had neither locks nor knobs; these had been stolen long ago and sold for scrap. Peculiar wet clumps, repulsive amalgams of rags and rotting refuse, were plastered to the tile floors, and the acrid ammonia stench of urine filled the air, leaving the hallway putrid.

On a wall, just at the foot of the staircase, someone had dutifully tacked a sign. It said: "Tenants Are Requested Not to Throw Garbage or Refuse of Any Kind Out of the Windows or in Halls. Order of Board of Health. Violators Are Subject to $25 Fine." In defiance, just below the sign, someone else had left an empty beer can in a brown paper bag. Rum and wine bottles, ranging in size from half pints to quarts, were tucked inside the metal window guard across the way.

The three detectives decided to split up. Carolann and Dominick would start on the top floor and work their way down. Carl would start on the bottom floor and work up. At the third floor, they would rejoin forces and compare notes. Anticipating the futility of a top-floor search, Carolann headed glumly for the stairs, wondering why on earth she had chosen this particular day to wear her high heels.

"C'mon, Carol, you can make it," Dominick said cheerily. "One foot at a time, one step after the other."

"Yeah, sure," said Carolann with a grimace. "Easy for you to say, Dom. You play racquetball. You're in shape."

A black man, one of the tenants, preceded the detectives up the stairs, humming to himself as he walked. Noticing the neatly dressed man and woman behind him, he turned and asked: "How y'all doin'? Y'all some of New York's Finest, ain't ya's?" There was just a tinge of sarcasm in his voice."

"Now how'd you know that?" Dominick asked slyly.

"Oh, I can tell, I can tell," laughed the man.

"You must be a detective," said Dominick.

"Yessir, I sho' is!" the man said, and he ducked into his apartment, out of sight.

As Carolann and Dominick continued higher, a cacophony of noises filled the stairwell. Whining babies. Barking dogs. Squealing children. Shouting parents. And, from almost every apartment, blasting television sets. Familiar sounds, the symphony of ghetto life.

On the top floor, the detectives curved around the bannister, gingerly sidestepping a mound of excrement, perhaps animal, perhaps human, but only partially covered by a piece of newspaper. Carolann walked up to one of the apartment doors, one without a latch, and rapped sharply.

At her touch, the unlocked door flew open, revealing a vacant apartment. She turned slightly and found herself staring at the bare buttocks of an old black wino, his trousers down around his ankles as he shuffled toward the bathroom.

"Oh, Jeez," she murmured with disgust. Stepping back hurriedly from the door, she motioned Dominick to take charge of this particular interrogation.

"Close dat door!" shouted the wino, suddenly realizing that he had an unwanted audience. Tripping clumsily, he struggled in vain to get his pants back up to a respectable level.

"We're the police," announced Dominick.

By now, the poor man was more startled than ever. "Wha'? Wha'? Whaddya want?" He was still trying to get a grip on his elusive trousers.

"Did you know the super here, the guy who got kidnaped?"

"Wha? I don't know nothin'. I don't know nothin'. Close dat door!"

"You don't know nothin'?"

"I don't know nothin'. *Now close dat door!*"

And slamming the door shut as hard as he could, Dominick obliged.

On the floor below, Carolann tried another apartment. At her knock, a little girl's voice answered. "Who is it?"

"Police Department."

"Who is it?"

"Police Department."

"Who is it?"

Carolann was growing exasperated. "Police Department."

"Who is it?"

This time, trying a new tack, Carolann asked: "Can we talk to your mother, dear?"

A murmur of voices followed, then the sound of shuffling

feet. Someone else had moved toward the door.

"Who is it?" asked a new female voice, an older one this time.

"Police Department," answered Carolann, echoing the familiar refrain.

"Who?"

"Police Department!" boomed Dominick, his voice deep and loud and his patience completely exhausted by this futile game.

Finally, some progress. "Wait a minute. I can't open the door. I ain't got no clothes on."

"Uh-oh," whispered Carolann. Remembering their encounter with the half-clad occupant upstairs, she murmured: "I'll get this one, Dom."

"That's okay," said Dominick with a teasing smile. "I'll get it, Carol."

At last, the door opened. A young woman was standing behind it, dressed in her bathrobe. Peeking out from behind her, a little girl with pigtails stared wide-eyed at the two detectives.

Unfortunately, the mother had little to add to the detectives' knowledge about the case. She had seen nothing. And heard nothing. The only thing she knew was that the super was "a bum."

"What kinda man is he, stealin' kids' beds?" she demanded to know. "Them kids got no place to sleep. All I can say is . . . whatever he got, he sure as hell deserved."

Carl was waiting at the third floor when Carolann and Dominick came down the stairs. "As usual," he reported, "nobody knows nothin'."

"So what else is new?" shrugged Dominick, and the three detectives trudged back toward their car.

No sooner had the detectives returned to the task force office when word came in of a fresh homicide, this one at an East Harlem social club. Buzzed out on booze and cocaine, an off-duty security guard and his friend had gotten into an argument with the social club's manager. The manager had pulled a knife. The security guard retaliated by pulling a gun. By the time the police arrived, the manager was lying outside on the sidewalk, a bullet hole in his chest. Carl Sgrizzi had an appointment to visit the district attorney's office, so Carolann and Dominick returned to Harlem to work this case by themselves, making the hospital morgue room their first stop.

Lying like a slab of beef on a roll-out steel drawer, the victim looked pallid and yellow in death. His eyes and his mouth were still open and his expression, the involuntary grimace of a corpse in rigor mortis, appeared to be one of astonishment. The shoe and sock had been removed from his right foot and the tag affixed to his big toe identified him only as "John Doe, male Hispanic." His pants pockets had been turned inside out by police officers looking for identification and his T-shirt had been yanked up around his shoulders, revealing a large gash in his chest, sutured up with black thread in neat, overlapping stitches. It was the incision the surgeons had made in a vain attempt to keep his heart beating.

Among the witnesses to the murder was a Puerto Rican woman who worked at the social club as a cleaning lady. When Carolann and Dominick returned to the Twenty-fifth Precinct from the morgue, she was sitting in the squad room, bawling like a baby. Several detectives already had tried to interview her, but without much success. Perhaps a woman detective could make more headway. Carolann drew the assignment.

Short, fat, and slovenly, the cleaning lady looked a pathetic sight in her tattered green sweater, filthy black slacks, and dirty sneakers, one of which had been slashed open at the instep to ease the pressure on her horribly swollen left foot. The foot was wrapped in a foul-looking bandage, moist and yellow from the festering ulcers underneath.

The wretched woman reeked of booze and her hands shook badly when she tried to speak. Her face was as wrinkled as old lizard's skin and when she moved her bloated cheeks, fumbling for the right words in her broken English, Carolann could see gums slapping against gums in her mouth. The poor hag had lost every last one of her teeth.

"Were you a friend of Ramon's?" Carolann asked the woman, deliberately neglecting to identify herself as a detective.

Terrified of the police, fearful of incriminating her friend Ramon, even though he already was dead, the old woman continued to sob. She nodded her head yes.

"Were you in the club when it happened?"

She nodded her head yes, again.

Carolann eased herself into the chair nearby. "Did you see your friend get shot?"

This time, the woman shook her head no, vigorously. But Carolann knew she was lying.

"Where were you when the shots were fired?"

The woman began to gesticulate with her hands, indicating some corner of the room in the social club. "Wall," she mumbled. "Near wall."

"What did you do when you heard the shots?"

Like a turtle withdrawing into its shell, the woman pulled both hands toward her belly, dropped her head and scrunched her shoulders together, as if the shots were flying again at that very moment. "I go down," she replied.

"What did you do then?"

With mime-like antics, the woman peeked up from her submerged position, raised her quivering hands over the top of an imaginary bar and, reaching for an imaginary bottle, poured herself an imaginary but very stiff drink.

"Vodka! Vodka!" she exclaimed, and she downed the drink in one desperate gulp. Hands still shaking, she poured herself another shot and swallowed that one, too.

Carolann pressed on. "When everyone else was outside, when the place was finally empty, what did you do?"

"I go out in front of bar and I take mop." She coiled her gnarled, scabby hands around an imaginary mop and began swishing it back and forth furiously, across the squad room floor. Her leathery face took on a look of urgency.

"What are you mopping?" asked Carolann.

"Blood."

"Mama," said Carolann, "where is the knife that was on the floor?"

The woman stared back, through frightened eyes. "No knife. I don't see knife."

"There had to be a knife. Did someone else come in? Did someone else take the knife?"

The woman was adamant. "No knife," she repeated. But Carolann knew it was just another lie.

* * *

There was one last stop to make before Carolann and Dominick finished their tour of duty.

When they pulled up to the social club in their unmarked car, the atmosphere outside was almost festive. Looking like participants at a ragtag block party, the winos sat on stoops and wooden crates, passing their bottles back and forth and gesturing wildly as they argued about who was the villain and who was the victim in the social club violence. The club itself was dark, except for an eerie purple light hanging just above the bar. The two detectives could gain access only by entering the side entrance, through the luncheonette next door.

At Carolann's request, one of the club's employees opened the front door to give them more light. According to witnesses' accounts, the shooting had occurred near the pool table. Carolann was down on one knee, searching for bullets and empty cartridges underneath, when she noticed a man walk in through the front door. Bearded and scruffy, he looked down at her through glassy eyes.

"You from the news?" he asked, his words slightly slurred.

"Nope," answered Carolann.

The wino cocked his head to one side, more puzzled than ever by the good-looking woman in front of him. "You a poh-*leese* offisuh?"

"Yup," admitted Carolann. "I'm one of those."

For a moment, the wino just stood there trying to make his rum-soaked brain comprehend. Then, reaching for the pint bottle in his hip pocket, he turned on his heels, stumbled back out the door and sighed:

"Jeeeeeeeeeeee-*sus!*"

Carolann rose slowly from the pool table, her eyes following the wino as he made his way unsteadily out the door. It was just a little snicker at first, breaking gradually into a chuckle, but before long, unable to stop herself, she burst into laughter.

"What's so funny?" asked Dominick, walking over from the other side of the room.

When she told him, he began to laugh too.

The blood, the death, the tragedy—those she might pretend to accept calmly and dispassionately. But there were still a few things about the job that Carolann Natale could never shrug off with hard-boiled nonchalance.

Even if she was a detective.

The Inspiring Stories of Women with Strength, Courage and Determination...

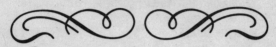

__HOMICIDE COP: THE TRUE STORY
  OF CAROLANN NATALE   05597-2/$2.95
Neal Hirschfield

__THE MAKING OF A
  WOMAN SURGEON   05034-3/$2.95
Elizabeth Morgan, M.D.

__MUGGABLE MARY   05042-4/$2.75
Detective Mary Glatzle with
Evelyn Fiore

__NURSE   05351-2/$2.95
Peggy Anderson

**Berkley Book Mailing Service
P.O. Box 690
Rockville Centre, NY 11570**

Please send me the above titles. I am enclosing $_____
(Please add 50¢ per copy to cover postage and handling). Send check or money
order—no cash or C.O.D.'s. Allow six weeks for delivery.

NAME_____

ADDRESS_____

CITY_____STATE/ZIP_____ *151*